ABC's OF RADIO & T.V.
BROADCASTING

ABC's OF
RADIO & T.V.
BROADCASTING

by

FARL J. WATERS

*With a specially written chapter for
the guidance of the English reader
by W. Oliver (G3XT)*

FOULSHAM-SAMS

TECHNICAL BOOKS

Published and distributed by
W. FOULSHAM & CO. LTD.,

SLOUGH   BUCKS   ENGLAND

W. FOULSHAM & CO., LTD.,
Yeovil Road, Slough, Bucks., England.

ABC's of RADIO AND T.V.

BROADCASTING

572 - 00572 - 5

Introduction Printed and Made in Great Britain
by East Midland Printing Company Limited, King's Lynn.
Balance Printed in U.S.A.

It is essential that the English reader should read this chapter.

There are certain points of difference between British and American electronic systems, therefore some of the information contained in any book of American origin dealing with electronic subjects usually needs re-orientating a little to fit the scene on this side of the ocean.

The present book is no exception to this rule, and this introductory chapter for English readers will deal with any points which might be confusing to beginners who do not happen to be familiar with the American aspects of the subjects covered in the main text.

Basic principles are much the same on both sides of the Atlantic, but details of practical application, as well as certain technical terms and so on, can vary quite a lot. These points of difference will be explained, more or less in the order in which they arise in the course of reading the American text which follows this introduction.

The first points to note are in regard to wavelength and frequency. In the United States, the long waveband is not used for broadcasting stations, only for other radio services. But here in Britain we have one broadcasting station in this waveband, which is of course BBC Radio 2 (formerly known as the Light Programme transmitter). There are also several other long-wave broadcasting stations in various European countries.

Sometimes we speak in terms of wavelength, sometimes in terms of frequency. Thus we speak of long, medium and short waves, as well as of microwaves. But some portions of the radio spectrum are more usually referred to in terms of frequency, hence the commonly-used abbreviations VHF (very high frequency) and UHF (ultra-high frequency). BBC frequency-modulated radio transmitters broadcast in the VHF band. Some TV transmitters also use frequencies that can be thus described; but others use much higher frequencies. BBC2, the 625-line and colour-service transmitters, are found in the UHF section of the spectrum.

Short waves, between say 10 and 100 metres roughly, exhibit special properties which make them suitable for world-wide communication when conditions are favourable. Anyone with an efficient short-wave receiver, or broadcast receiver incorporating short-wave reception facilities, can pick up programmes from countries all over the world, as well as many other kinds of transmission, including messages from amateur stations.

In the section headed "Modulation", the author says: "It is necessary to place or load something on to the radio-frequency wave to make it useful." One exception to this rule is worth noting: if an unmodulated radio-frequency wave is "keyed" into the dots and dashes that form Morse Code letters and figures, this is a case in which it can be made useful without having to "place or load something" on to it. An exception which proves the rule!

In the section headed "Transducers" the author says that a transducer changes one form of energy into a different form. The present writer feels, however, that the action of a transducer may be more readily and accurately visualised if one thinks of it as translating rather than changing. For example, a microphone translates variations in sound waves into corresponding variations in electric current.

Both the sound and the current exist simultaneously and independently in two totally different mediums—air and wire, or some other conducting substance. When the sound waves vary, the microphone makes the electric current passing through it vary in sympathy.

In the chapter on Video Modulating Signals, the section headed "Scanning" is a portion of the text which must be re-orientated to fit the British television system and our electricity mains. The latter alternate at 50 Hz (cycles per second), therefore the reference to the American standard of 60 Hz must be amended accordingly, and this of course in turn affects the question of synchronisation.

Moreover, in the matter of line standards the American system differs from ours. The reference to 525 lines relates to the American standard. Here in Britain, at the time of writing, a much more complicated situation exists; two different line standards are in use—405 lines for BBC1 and ITV, but 625 lines for BBC2 and its colour transmissions. Two different systems of modulation — Amplitude Modulation (AM) and Frequency Modulation (FM)— are also in use simultaneously on the different wavebands.

All this makes British TV sets much more complex, and less standardised, than American ones. But these arrangements are not necessarily permanent and changes may be anticipated in the future.

As regards colour television, the method used at present by American stations is known as the NTSC system. Here in Britain we are using a system based on the German one known as PAL.

The chapter on Carrier Origin also needs a little re-orientation, as here again the references are to American television channels, etc.

References to the FCC or Federal Communications Commission relate to the authority in the United States which deals with such matters as radio and TV licencing, transmitting regulations and everything of that sort, in much the same way as our GPO Radio Department. But regulations in the States differ considerably in some respects from those in force over here.

The chapter on Power Supplies gives typical examples of American power-supply units. The input voltage shown is that of American domestic mains running at about 117 volts a-c. This is only about half the British standard voltage, which in most places nowadays is rated at about 230-240 volts a-c. On some American supplies, a voltage of over 200 is available, but the supply is arranged differently from ours and as the book explains consists virtually of two 117-volt circuits in series with the centre point earthed.

You will notice a few technical terms which differ somewhat

from the British equivalents. For example, aerials are described as antennas, valves are termed tubes, and an earthing connection is known as a ground. But the majority of electronic terms are the same on both sides of the Atlantic.

Preface

In this supermarket era, the origination of a product or a service is often overlooked or forgotten. To some extent this is true of radio and television—a simple twist of the dial picks off the desired broadcast from the "shelf." Even the electronics student may pass over the origination of the broadcast and not fully understand it. This book is meant to provide a basic knowledge of broadcast methods, circuits, and related equipment.

The text begins with the fundamental principles of electromagnetic wave propagation and its modulated forms. Other sections are devoted to the circuits and equipment used to produce, control, and monitor both the modulating signal and the carrier signal; to the circuits used to load the modulating signal onto the carrier; and to the various systems of radiating antennas. For example, the chapter on audio modulating signals discusses the basic form of audio signals, their various sources, amplifiers, controls, meters, and monitoring circuits.

Block diagrams are used extensively to relate the various pieces of equipment, while simplified circuit diagrams illustrate the discussion. Primary points are emphasized by review questions at the end of each chapter, and the answers provided at the back of the book give added assistance to the student.

In this book an effort has been made to give the student a factual, but simple, introduction to the technical side of broadcasting. While the text is not complete enough to provide the knowledge for passing the FCC examinations required to become a broadcast engineer, it can readily serve as vocational guidance toward that goal.

FARL JACOB WATERS

Contents

1

Fundamentals
of Broadcasting

Ever since Biblical days tares, or weeds, have plagued the farmer. Many weeds utilize a springlike action to throw out their seeds. In addition, the seed is attached to a fluffy structure that floats in the wind. Thus, the seed is the cargo, or *load*, of this fluffy structure, or *carrier*. Similarly, the signal emitted or thrown out by a broadcast station is a composite of the carrier and its load. The carrier is a high-frequency electromagnetic wave, while the load is a wave varying according to sound or light waves.

ELECTROMAGNETIC INDUCTION

Every magnetic material develops a field of force which may be described by *lines of magnetic force*. An alternating current, i.e., a movement of electrons which reverses direction, develops a magnetic force that travels outward from the conductor as the current increases (Figs. 1-1A and B), and

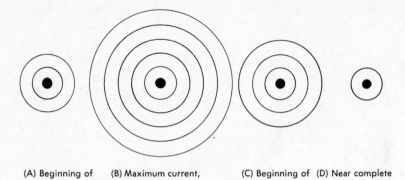

(A) Beginning of
expansion.

(B) Maximum current,
maximum expansion.

(C) Beginning of
collapse.

(D) Near complete
collapse.

Fig. 1-1. Variation of magnetic lines about a conductor carrying pulsating current.

that reverses direction as the current decreases (Figs. 1-1C and D). The magnetic lines produced by an alternating current thus pulsate.

If a second conductor is placed within that pulsating magnetic field, the magnetic lines cut that second conductor. This concentration of magnetic lines passing through the second conductor causes a flow of electrons, or a current, within the second conductor. Stated more directly, the current of the first conductor *induces* a current in the second conductor. The current induced in the second conductor generates a magnetic field opposed to that of the current in the first conductor. The resultant field of the current in the first conductor is shown in Fig. 1-2.

However, the constant magnetic field of a direct current will not move and cut the second conductor, and therefore it

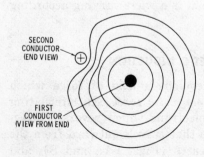

SECOND
CONDUCTOR
(END VIEW)

FIRST
CONDUCTOR
(VIEW FROM END)

Fig. 1-2. Magnetic lines, produced by current in first conductor, cutting a second conductor.

will not induce a current. Thus, an induced current can be developed only by a moving magnetic field.

FREQUENCY AND WAVELENGTH

An electromagnetic field moves along the length of a conductor at the speed of light (186,000 miles per second). An electromagnetic wave having a frequency of 100 hertz, where 1 hertz (Hz) = 1 cycle per second, moves 1860 miles during the time of one cycle (0.01 second). Thus, an electromagnetic wave with a frequency of 100 Hz is said to have a *wavelength* of 1860 miles, or 3,000,000 meters. And since a 200-Hz wave completes its cycle in one-half the time of a 100-Hz wave, the wavelength of a 200-Hz wave is one-half of that of the 100-Hz wave, i.e., 1,500,000 meters. Thus, the following formula may be written:

$$\text{Wavelength} = \frac{300,000,000 \text{ meters}}{\text{Frequency (Hz)}}$$

Electromagnetic wavelengths are classified in four groups: long waves, medium waves, short waves, and microwaves. *Long waves* are those having wavelengths greater than 500 meters and thus having frequencies below 600,000 Hz. Between 188 and 500 meters are the *medium waves*, with frequencies from 600,000 to 1,600,000 Hz, the standard broadcast band. Waves with wavelengths shorter than 188 meters are known as *short waves*, while *microwaves* is the term given to those waves with wavelengths of less than one meter. Our f-m broadcast stations operate with frequencies between 88 and 108 MHz, or wavelengths of about 3 meters, while the wavelengths of broadcasts from television stations range from about ½ meter to 6 meters.

STANDING WAVES

An electromagnetic wave is analogous to a wave of water. Waves caused by a disturbance at one end of a long canal travel uninterrupted along the full length of that canal until they dissipate. If a dam is placed at some point in the canal, waves striking the dam will react to produce a second wave that moves in the opposite direction. Very similarly, an energy wave that suddenly comes to the end of the conductor will be blocked and reflected.

Fig. 1-3 shows the initial wave moving to the right, while the wave moving to the left is a reflected wave. By addition of the instantaneous values of the initial wave and the reflected wave, a resultant wave is found. This resultant of the initial plus the reflected waves remains in the same position (though varying in amplitude) and therefore is considered a *standing wave*. A standing wave, while not moving along the length of the con-

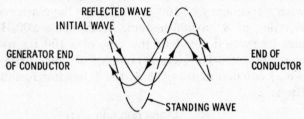

Fig. 1-3. Standing-wave analysis.

ductor, will vary in magnitude at its nonzero points. If the conductor is terminated in a load or an impedance that absorbs the initial wave, there can be no reflected wave and hence no standing wave.

RADIATION

Although the standing wave is the resultant of two electromagnetic energy waves, it does have a corresponding magnetic field that varies in intensity. When currents of frequencies above 200,000 Hz are fed to a conductor, a form of electromagnetic energy known as *radio waves* is radiated from the conductor. Radio waves comprise electrostatic and electromagnetic fields of energy which move through space at the speed of light. The characteristics of these waves are such that current will be induced into any conductor they cross. The conductor radiating these waves is the *transmitting antenna*, while the *receiving antenna* is that conductor in which the current is induced.

The wavelengths at frequencies below 200,000 Hz are too long to produce radiation practically. Waves at frequencies between 200,000 and 500,000 Hz have a tendency to disperse—in contrast to the extremely short waves of light, which travel in a straight line. Long waves tend to curve around obstructions and to a degree follow the curvature of the earth, thereby increasing the communication range.

Thus, long-wave radiation is generally used for those radio applications which must be dependable (transoceanic telephone, radionavigation of ships and aircraft, etc.). Although we normally think of the standard broadcast station as being dependable, it is limited to a primary service area having a radius of about 30 miles. Greater radiated power will extend that area, but the communication range does not increase in direct proportion to the power increase.

Waves traveling upward from the earth's surface are known as *sky waves*. Under the proper conditions, these sky waves may be refracted (bent) back to the earth many miles from their point of origin. Reception of these refracted sky waves is somewhat unpredictable. However, sky-wave or *skip reception*, as it is sometimes called, at frequencies up to 30,000,000 Hz is generally good enough for extensive commercial communication. At frequencies above 30,000,000 Hz the sky wave is refracted very little and does not normally return to earth. Thus, our television and f-m stations, operating at frequencies above 50,000,000 Hz, are generally limited to a primary service area having a radius of less than 50 miles.

MODULATION

Radiated radio-frequency waves travel through space and thus may be considered as electric vehicles. As with the vehicles, it is necessary to place or load something onto the radio-frequency wave to make it useful. Being an abstract thing that does not excite any of our five senses, the radio-frequency wave has a load that is also an abstract thing—some other electromotive force. And, just as a weight placed on a mechanical vehicle affects its speed or its power, the "load" on a radio-frequency wave can alter either the amplitude or the frequency of the wave.

This "load" of the radio-frequency wave is commonly an electromotive force that varies as a sound wave or other variation providing some form of intelligence. With this intelligence, i.e., the *modulating signal*, the radio-frequency wave is a *modulated wave*. The circuit used to combine the radio-frequency carrier wave with the modulating wave is the *modulator*. When the modulator causes the carrier wave to vary in amplitude, the result is *amplitude modulation*. *Frequency modulation* occurs when the modulator causes the carrier wave to deviate from its normal frequency.

RECEPTION

Although this book is primarily concerned with the broadcasting or transmission of modulated waves, it will be worthwhile to review briefly the basic method of receiving and detecting that modulated wave. Fig. 1-4 is a block diagram of the commonly used superheterodyne receiver. When the modulated radio-frequency wave cuts the receiving antenna, a current is

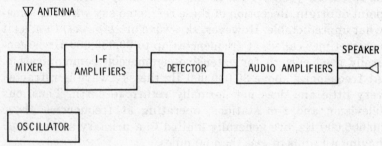

Fig. 1-4. Block diagram of a-m superheterodyne receiver.

induced. This develops a radio-frequency voltage which is then mixed with a second radio-frequency voltage produced by the local oscillator within the mixer section. Ordinarily the mixer section and local oscillator are combined in a converter section. The output of the mixer or converter contains both the received frequency and the local-oscillator frequency, as well as their sum and their difference frequencies. Proper alignment of the local oscillator sets the difference frequency at a fixed value for all received frequencies. This fixed difference frequency is the *intermediate frequency*. Futher increase in amplitude is obtained by action of the intermediate-frequency (i-f) amplifier sections (or stages). Separation of the intelligence or modulating signal from the i-f carrier occurs in the detector or discriminator stages, while audio amplifiers (or video amplifiers and sync circuits) bring the intelligence to proper utilization.

REVIEW QUESTIONS

1. Discuss briefly the principle of electromagnetic induction. Will direct current produce an induced current?
2. What is a wavelength? What is the wavelength of a 1,000,000-Hz radio wave?
3. What is a standing wave?
4. Name the two types of fields produced by radiated radio waves.
5. What is the average radius of a standard broadcast station service area? Of a television station?
6. What is the modulating signal? The modulated wave?
7. Does amplitude modulation cause a deviation in frequency?

2

Audio Modulating Signals

Not much study is needed to discover that railroad cars and trucks are designed for a definite type of load. A car or truck for hauling cattle cannot be used for transporting oil, gasoline, or other liquids, and neither type can be considered satisfactory for human cargo. Thus, it is necessary to study and understand the nature and origin of the load. Similarly, the nature and origin of the load or modulating signal of the composite broadcast wave must be studied and understood. In addition, the preparation or handling of the modulating signal is very important.

AUDIO-WAVE CHARACTERISTICS

Sound or audio waves are vibrations of the air. It is necessary for these air waves to strike against the eardrum (Fig. 2-1) for us to perceive external sounds. The action of the eardrum and parts of the inner ear produce electrical waves that travel to the brain. A *fundamental* sound wave consists of a series of rarefactions and compressions whose density follows

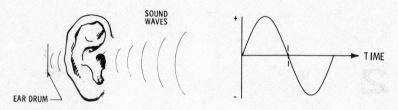

Fig. 2-1. Sound wave acting on the ear.   Fig. 2-2. Sine wave.

the pattern of a trigonometric sine wave (Fig. 2-2). However, many sounds are combinations of a fundamental wave and its *harmonics*, a harmonic being a multiple of a fundamental's frequency. For example, Fig. 2-3A shows a fundamental wave having a frequency of 100 Hz, while its 200-Hz harmonic wave is shown in Fig. 2-3B. Added together, the fundamental and

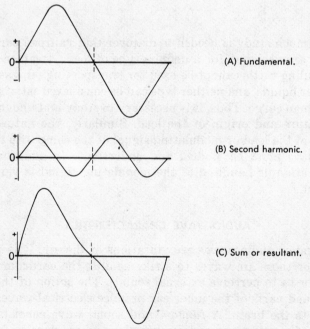

(A) Fundamental.

(B) Second harmonic.

(C) Sum or resultant.

Fig. 2-3. Addition of waves of different frequencies.

16

the harmonic give the wave shown in Fig. 2-3C. The human ear responds to frequencies ranging from about 30 to 20,000 Hz.

TRANSDUCERS

Fundamentally, a transducer is any device that changes one form of energy into a different form. Audio, or sound, transducers change sound waves to electrical waves or electrical waves to sound waves. The basic audio transducer is the *microphone*. Much like the human ear, the microphone has a diaphragm linked to some generating device that produces electrical waves similar to those developed within the human ear. Therefore, the microphone is an attempt to duplicate the ear.

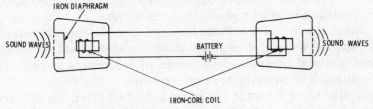

Fig. 2-4. An early telephone.

Alexander Graham Bell made the first attempt to duplicate the ear with a very thin iron diaphragm within an electromagnetic field (Fig. 2-4). As sound waves cause the diaphragm to vibrate, the current similarly varies and, in turn, causes a second diaphragm to vibrate and reproduce the original sound wave.

In broadcasting, two types of microphones are commonly used: the crystal or ceramic type and the dynamic type. Fig. 2-5 illustrates the working principles of both the crystal and the dynamic microphones. With a high impedance the crystal microphone can operate directly into any amplifier circuit and has an output of at least −60 db over most of the audio-frequency range, viz, 30 to 15,000 Hz. The dynamic-type microphone has a good frequency response from 30 to 15,000 Hz, an output of −50 db, and impedances of 50, 150, 250 ohms, or higher.

Still another type, with ratings similar to the dynamic type, is the ribbon, or velocity, microphone. The ribbon-type microphone has the disadvantage of producing unwanted noises

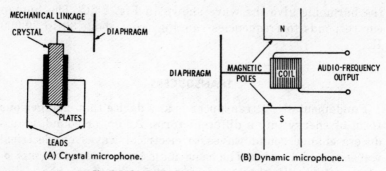

(A) Crystal microphone.   (B) Dynamic microphone.

Fig. 2-5. Construction of two microphone types.

when moved. And while the microphones in the sound studio are usually mounted on fairly stationary stands or booms, those used in television studios are moved about almost constantly on overhead booms or on cords about the neck.

Since the cost of live musicians and other talent is generally beyond the budget of most broadcasters, such talent or broadcast material is obtained by means of recordings or network facilities. The primary type of recording is the phonographic disc, like those found in the home, but often given special care in manufacturing. In years past, 16-inch-diameter *transcription* recordings were used extensively along with prepared scripts (supplied by the manufacturer) that were to be read by the announcer. Such transcription recordings have an aluminum base coated with a wax substance into which four to six musical numbers are cut from the center outward (the reverse of standard recordings) on each side. The speed of these transcriptions, like many of the modern microgroove recordings, is 33⅓ rpm, while other modern recordings use a speed of 45 rpm.

Naturally the turntable used in the sound studio provides for all sizes and speeds of disc recordings and has mechanical features better than those found in home equipment. A diamond-tipped stylus, or needle, with an electromagnetic unit forms the dynamic-type phonograph pickup used. The entire turntable-pickup unit is commonly built into a desk-height cabinet that may also house frequency-compensating networks and preamplifiers.

For announcements, commercials, etc., that are to be recorded locally and played repeatedly, the tape recording and tape cartridge are of importance. Tape recording is also used extensively for delaying the broadcasting of program material. Tape recorders use a ¼-inch-wide acetate or *Mylar* tape coated with iron oxide. As the tape is pulled across the gap between two laminated electromagnetic poles energized by an audio-frequency current, the iron oxide becomes magnetized in proportion to the current. When the tape moves at a speed of 7½ ips (inches per second), the frequency response is good for nearly the entire audio range. Playback is accomplished by pulling the tape over the same or similar electromagnetic poles.

In the control room the tape recorders are usually mounted vertically in equipment racks, and two or more will be present to permit recording and playback at the same time as well as for flexibility. The announcer's booth often has one or more tape-cartridge players. The tape cartridge consists of two small reels of tape encased in plastic that is quickly set into the machine for playing 5-second, 10-second, 30-second, or 60-second announcements, etc. Such tape cartridges play and rewind almost automatically in order to be easily handled by the announcer.

TRANSMISSION LINES

Remote and network transmission lines also provide means of bringing program material into the audio studio. American Telephone and Telegraph and the local telephone companies own, maintain, and lease these transmission lines to the broadcast station and to the networks. Most of these lines are of a better quality—providing better frequency response—than the common twisted-pair telephone lines serving our homes. Broadcasters commonly have two or more such lines coming into the control room from the telephone-company building, where connections can be made to any desired point. The telephone company specifies that to avoid crosstalk the absolute maximum should not exceed 6 dbm* where the better-quality lines are being used. But because there are still older-type lines in use the telephone company advises that a 3-dbm maximum be taken as a general limit.

---

*Dbm is the number of decibels above (or below) the standard reference of 1 vu (volume unit) or 0.001 watt across 600 ohms. Therefore 3 dbm is equivalent to 0.002 watt.

AMPLIFIERS

Because each of the preceding methods of developing audio current waves has a very low level output, there must be amplification. For example, the amplitude modulation of a 1000-watt transmitter may require 500 watts of audio power, with a peak of 2500 volts. While a large portion of this audio power will be developed by the modulating amplifier (modulator) as a portion of the transmitter system, the studio equipment may be expected to bring the audio up to at least the 8-vu level. Then, since the transmitter is often as much as 10 or 20 miles from the studio, the audio current is fed to the transmitter by means of telephone-company lines.

Microphone, turntable, and tape-recorder outputs are fed into preamplifiers to increase the signal from about 0.001 volt to 1 or 2 volts (see Fig. 2-6). As shown by the block diagram of Fig. 2-6, a potentiometer or "fader" follows each preamplifier. To be more exact, the fader is a variable attenuator similar

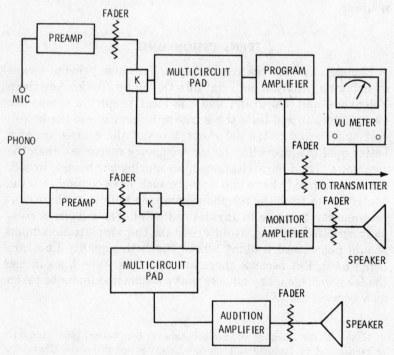

Fig. 2-6. Block diagram of audio studio equipment.

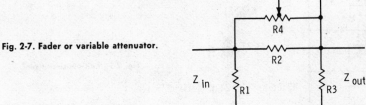

Fig. 2-7. Fader or variable attenuator.

to the circuit of Fig. 2-7. The preamplifiers have a two-stage r-c coupled circuit using pentode tubes or transistors to give the best frequency response (Fig. 2-8). Such preamplifiers are commonly built into the control console.

So that more than one source of audio currents—say, two microphones, one microphone and a phonograph pickup, a microphone and a remote line, or any other combination—may be used at the same time, the various outputs of the preamplifiers are combined within a multiple-circuit pad. The multiple-circuit pad (Fig. 2-9) matches the impedances of the many preamplifiers to the input impedance of the program amplifier.

In contrast to the preamplifier, the *program amplifier* (Fig. 2-10) is a balanced circuit having one or two stages on each side of ground. This balanced arrangement has the advantage of eliminating the distortion of even harmonics. Accordingly the balanced circuits, as shown by Fig. 2-10, are operated as class-B amplifiers, while the unbalanced are class-A. Of utmost importance is the portion of the program-amplifier output that goes to the transmitter. However, a larger portion may be fed to the monitoring amplifier and possibly to network lines. Con-

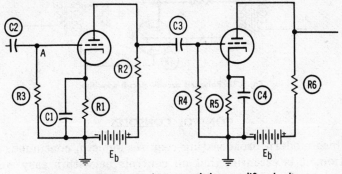

Fig. 2-8. Resistance-capacitance coupled preamplifier circuit.

21

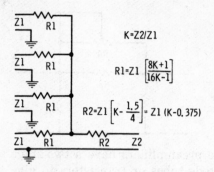

$$K = Z2/Z1$$

$$R1 = Z1 \left[\frac{8K+1}{16K-1}\right]$$

Fig. 2-9. Multiple-circuit pad.

$$R2 = Z1 \left[K - \frac{1.5}{4}\right] = Z1\,(K-0.375)$$

trol of the program-amplifier output is by means of another variable attenuator, and it is measured by the vu meter.

To check the output of the program amplifier, other than by visual observation of the vu meter, it is necessary to hear the equivalent sound. Therefore a portion of the program-amplifier output is fed to a *monitor amplifier*. A monitor amplifier is a power amplifier providing enough power to drive a number of speakers. In addition to the monitoring speaker in the control room, speakers may be desired in the various studios and offices about the station. With low distortion and extremely good frequency responses, the class-B push-pull monitor amplifier is capable of providing an adequate sampling. Fig. 2-6 indicates the relation between the program and monitor amplifiers.

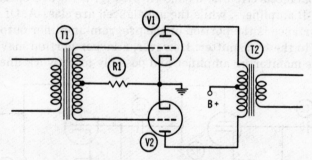

Fig. 2-10. Balanced circuit—class-B amplifier.

CONTROL CONSOLES

Since modern broadcasting requires smooth, continuous operation, it is essential that all controls be within easy reach and sight. In addition to being able to see the controls and

Fig. 2-11. Studio console located on desk.

meters, it is also essential for the engineer to see the action within the studio. Accordingly, controls—the various attenuators and switches—and meters are located on a sloping panel referred to as the *control console* (Fig. 2-11). Having a width of five feet and mounted just below the studio window and at desk height, as in Fig. 2-11, the control console is very convenient. Of course, there can be variations and additions to this basic form of the control console.

Fig. 2-12 shows the front panel of a typical control console. At the upper left, one row of push buttons (1) selects the source of audio to be auditioned, while a second row (2) selects the source to be monitored. The lever-type switch (3) below

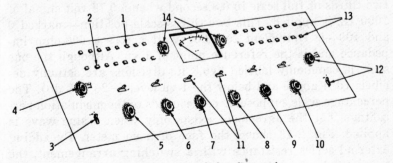

Fig. 2-12. Front panel of studio console.

these buttons selects the audition circuit or method desired: regular audition-amplifier circuit, earphones, or monitor amplifier. Knob (4) is the knob with pointer and numbers 0–20 for adjusting the monitor-amplifier output level. Knobs (5), (6), (7), (8), (9), and (10) adjust the attenuators following the preamplifiers for the microphones, phonograph pickups, and incoming lines. Above each of these preamplifier attenuators are lever-type switches (11), for audition, off, and program.

The attenuator knob and lever-type switch (12) at the far right control the output level of the program amplifier and select the line to the transmitter desired. Added versatility and convenience are provided by the two rows of push buttons at the upper right of the console (13); they permit selection of the inputs to the preamplifiers of attenuators (9) and (10). Thus, using the attenuator (8) for the announcer's (disc jockey's) microphone and using attenuators (9) and (10) for phonograph pickups, tape playbacks, and remote lines simplifies the operation.

In the upper-center portion of the console are the meter(s) and small rotary switches for selecting the range and the circuit to be metered (items marked "14" in Fig. 2-12). The space behind the front panel of the console is occupied by the various amplifiers, attenuators, and pads shown by the block diagram of Fig. 2-6.

VU METERS

Basically the vu meter is a rectifier-type voltmeter with a 3900-ohm impedance damped so that the pointer will come to two-thirds of full scale in 0.3 second when a 0.78-volt signal of 1000 Hz is applied. This two-thirds-scale position—marked 0 and 100—is equivalent to 0.001 watt across a 600-ohm impedance and is the reference point of 1 vu. Although the one scale is ocmmonly labeled "vu," its divisions are actually decibels (db) above and below the 1-vu level (−20 to 3 db). The percentage scale supposedly corresponds to modulation percentage, but the agreement exists only when a sine wave is applied. Fig. 2-13 shows the face of a vu meter. By adding external series resistance with a switching arrangement, the reference level of the vu meter can be changed from 4 to 24

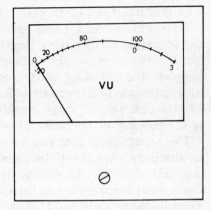

Fig. 2-13. Face of vu meter.

dbm.* Often, on the control console, the vu meter will also be used for rapid checking of various anode or transistor currents of the amplifier circuits.

PATCH PANELS

The word "patch" is defined as "to mend or to repair in a temporary fashion." In broadcasting, patching is a temporary form of repair or alternation using a prearranged system of cords, plugs, and jacks. The plug has two prongs consisting of a sleeve and a tip separated by an insulating ring (Fig. 2-14). Fig. 2-14 also shows a pair of jacks for the two-pronged plug, with the spring contacts acting as switches to make or to break the circuits. That is, the plug tips push against the V-shaped contacts to open the circuits between A and A′ and between B and B′. Actually the jacks will likely have three make-and-break switching combinations.

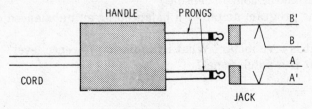

Fig. 2-14. Two-prong plug and jack.

---

*Dbm is the number of decibels above (or below) the standard reference of 1 vu or 0.001 watt across 600 ohms.

In multiple rows of 12 pairs of jacks per row and mounted in an equipment rack, these jacks form a *patch panel*. Shielded and insulated cords having lengths of one, two, three, and five feet and two-pronged plugs at each end, known as *patch cords*, complete the patching equipment. By wiring the various remote, network, and transmitter lines and the various amplifiers into the patch panel, many combinations exist for alternations or for making quick checks when trouble develops.

The sound studio also uses many other components classified as auxiliary equipment. Included are the cuing circuits, the talk-back circuits, the on-the-air lights, the indicator lights, and a great many relays to turn on lights and cut off speakers when the lever switches (11) on the studio console activate a microphone, etc.

REVIEW QUESTIONS

1. What are audio waves?
2. What is an audio transducer? Name three types used in audio studios.
3. Are the grooves of the standard disc record cut from the center outward?
4. What is a transcription recording?
5. At what speed does the tape move through the tape recorder, for the best response?
6. What is the purpose of tape-cartridge players?
7. How are telephone-company lines utilized by the broadcast stations?
8. Name, in order, the amplifiers of the usual sound-studio equipment.
9. Describe the control console.
10. Is the program amplifier a balanced or an unbalanced circuit?
11. What is a vu meter? What is its basic reference level?
12. What is a patch panel?

3

Video Modulating Signals

Next to the sensation of sound, that of sight, or seeing, is probably most pleasing to many people. Similarly, the second most desirable load for the television composite broadcast wave is the sight wave—the *video wave*.

VIDEO-WAVE CHARACTERISTICS

The sight or seeing of external objects is due to various light rays acting on the retina of the eye. Our primary light source would have to be considered the sun, while flames and electric lamps are other light sources. But a large portion of the light reaching the eye is reflected light from the objects in the area. Initially the white-light source contains all colors, while an object may absorb most or all of that white light. A black object will absorb all light, but a red object will reflect the red portion of a white light, a blue object will reflect the blue portion of white light, etc. Thus, most of the light reaching the eye is reflected from objects that are neither white nor black. The retina is covered with a multitude of light-sensitive

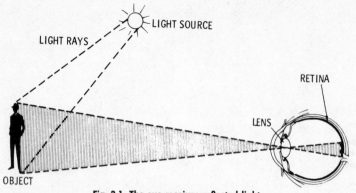

Fig. 3-1. The eye receives reflected light.

nerve cells, some responding to red, some to blue, some to green, and so on. White-light rays striking a group of these nerve cells will excite all of them and produce the sensation of a white area. Fig. 3-1 shows the cross section of an eye receiving reflected light waves. The black area reflects none of the light and excites none of the retina's nerve cells, while light reflected from the white area excites only those cells

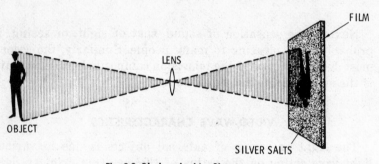

Fig. 3-2. Black and white film camera.

sensitive to white light. In black and white photography the silver salts, replacing the eye retina, turn dark in direct proportion to the amount of light. Thus reflected white light will turn the silver salts completely black, while light reflected from colored objects has less effect on the silver salts (see Fig. 3-2). A *negative*, with the originally white areas appearing black and the black appearing white, is formed in this manner. Color photography makes use of different elements that react to the various colored light waves.

The eye and its retina are almost duplicated by an electronic camera for television broadcasting. The electronic retina (Fig. 3-3), has a surface of minute photosensitive globules (beads) insulated from a metal backplate. Each photosensitive globule forms a capacitance with the backplate and loses electrons to become positively charged in proportion to the intensity of light acting on it. That is, a globule receiving white-light rays will become very positively charged, while light rays reflected from a colored surface produce less positive charges. As these

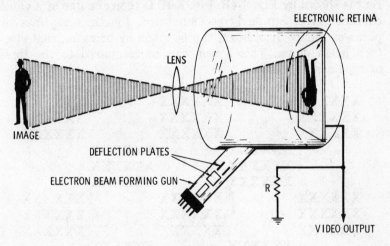

Fig. 3-3. Television camera tube.

globules acquire positive charges, the backplate takes an equal but opposite negative charge—equaling the accumulative total of all globule charges.

Electrons formed into a beam and directed at the photosensitive globules tend to replace electrons lost by the effect of light. Then the backplate loses an equal number of electrons through resistor R of Fig. 3-3. Accordingly when the electron beam hits a photosensitive globule activated by white light, the electron flow through R is maximum. Between this maximum current developed by white light and the black level of zero current are the current levels of all other colors and tints. That is, if the scene reflected through various lenses onto the surface is a black and white checkerboard, the horizontally moved electron beam will produce a current wave of square pulses. Fig. 3-4A indicates the checkerboard scene and the

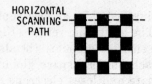

HORIZONTAL
SCANNING
PATH

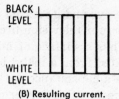

(A) Visual checkerboard pattern.　　　　(B) Resulting current.

Fig. 3-4. Visual and video signals.

horizontal path of the electron beam, while the resulting current is shown by Fig. 3-4B. Fig. 3-4B is then one line of a video current wave. Similarly second, third, fourth, etc., lines or paths of the electron beam can be made by bringing that electron beam down. This action can be compared to the lines of type across a page:

```
XXXXXX        XXXXXX        XXXXXX
XXXXXX        XXXXXX        XXXXXX
XXXXXX        XXXXXX        XXXXXX
      XXXXXX        XXXXXX
      XXXXXX        XXXXXX
      XXXXXX        XXXXXX
XXXXXX        XXXXXX        XXXXXX
XXXXXX        XXXXXX        XXXXXX
XXXXXX        XXXXXX        XXXXXX
      XXXXXX        XXXXXX
      XXXXXX        XXXXXX
      XXXXXX        XXXXXX
```

However, if the squares were red and black, the contrast would be less pronounced, as shown by the video current wave of Fig. 3-5, and the equivalent lines of type would be as follows:

```
XXXXX · · · · XXXXX · · · · · XXXXX
XXXXX · · · · XXXXX · · · · XXXXX
XXXXX · · · · XXXXX · · · · · XXXXX
· · · · · XXXXX · · · · · XXXXX · · · ·
· · · · · XXXXX · · · · · XXXXX · · · ·
· · · · · XXXXX · · · · · XXXXX · · · · ·
XXXXX · · · · XXXXX · · · · · XXXXX
XXXXX · · · · · XXXXX · · · · · XXXXX
XXXXX · · · · · XXXXX · · · · · XXXXX
```

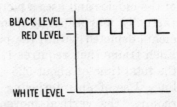

Fig. 3-5. Video signal of black and red checkerboard.

BLACK LEVEL —
RED LEVEL —

WHITE LEVEL —

SCANNING

In the reading of this book the eyes are moved horizontally back and forth across the page and vertically downward one line at a time. And when the bottom of the page is reached, an upward vertical movement is made to the top of the next page. This action is a form of *scanning*. In effect, the electron beam (Fig. 3-3) scans the electronic retina by moving horizontally back and forth and vertically downward one line at a time. Fig. 3-3 shows horizontal- and vertical-deflection plates using electrostatic forces to move the electron beam for scanning. However, scanning can be, and usually is, accomplished by electromagnetic deflection coils mounted about the neck of the camera tube or electronic eye. The camera tube of Fig. 3-3 is an enclosed vacuum containing the electronic retina, the electron beam forming "gun," and the internal deflection plates or the external electromagnetic deflection coils.

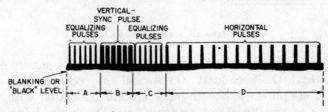

Fig. 3-6. Television synchronizing pulses.

Pulses of voltage to the deflection plates or pulses of current to the deflection coils produce the desired scanning movements. While the ideal shape of these "horizontal" pulses is square, Fig. 3-6 shows that they are actually wider at the bottom than at the top. The back-and-forth movement is produced by the horizontal pulses lasting for 0.0000032 second at intervals of 0.000064 second. Upward movement is accomplished by the vertical-sync pulses of 0.000027-second duration at intervals of 0.000032 second. Television follows some of the principles

31

of the movies and uses a picture or frame rate of 30 per second (actually, movies use 24 frames per second) to make any movements depicted within the pictures seem smoothly continuous. Each frame then requires 1/30 or 0.0333 second, which is also the total time of about 525 horizontal pulses or 525 horizontal lines. Use of an interlacing pattern for these horizontal lines requires the vertical movement to occur twice during each frame or once each 1/60 of a second—corresponding to the rate of the alternating-current supply. Thus, the rates of the

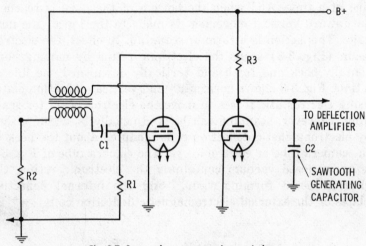

Fig. 3-7. Sawtooth generator using a triode.

deflection pulses are synchronized with the 60-Hz supply current at both the broadcast station and the receiver. Fig. 3-7 shows a simplified sawtooth-pulse circuit associated with the scanning or synchronizing system. Actually, at the television broadcasting station, the scanning or synchronizing system is a complex combination of crystal oscillators, multivibrators, pulse generators, and monitoring equipment.

The complete video modulating signal is a combination of the scanning pulses and the video current wave. The video modulating wave is much more complex than the audio modulating wave, and it has a frequency range with a 4.5-MHz width. Fig. 3-8 shows a line of video current wave between two horizontal scanning pulses and their relation to the black and white levels.

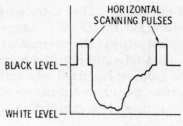

HORIZONTAL
SCANNING PULSES

BLACK LEVEL —

WHITE LEVEL —

Fig. 3-8. Video current signal with horizontal scanning pulses.

VIDEO TRANSDUCER

Just as the microphone is the primary transducer for changing sound waves into audio current waves, the television camera is the basic transducer for changing light rays into video current waves. The heart of the television camera is the camera tube with its electronic retina, its electron beam forming gun, and deflecting plates or coils. Linking the light rays with the camera tube is a system of lenses providing for the proper locating and focusing of the image on the electronic retina. The usual studio camera has a turret of three different lenses turned by an electric motor at the will of the cameraman (Fig. 3-9). Other cameras have a continuously adjustable lens system for "zooming" into or away from close-ups.

The camera unit also houses auxiliary circuits—pulse generators, high-voltage circuits used to form the electron beam,

FRONT   REAR

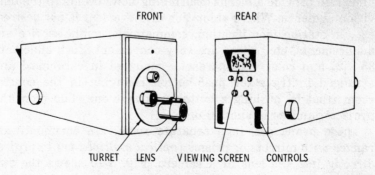

TURRET   LENS   VIEWING SCREEN   CONTROLS

Fig. 3-9. Television camera.

and so on. Controls for all of these circuits, as well as a viewing screen like that on the home receiver, are found at the rear of the camera. They include brightness, contrast, focus, vertical and horizontal positioning, and scanning controls. The focus control adjusts the sharpness of the electron beam within the camera tube and provides means of correcting inadequacies of the more or less fixed lens system. A multiple-conductor cable carries power and synchronizing signals to the camera and a complete video modulating signal away from the camera.

VIDEO TAPE RECORDERS

Operating on the same principle as the audio tape recorder, the video tape recorder uses a 1-inch-wide iron-oxide coated tape moving at a rate of 10 ips. A portion of the width of the tape is used for the audio portion of the broadcast, while the other portion is used for video recording. The video tape recorder has much the same uses as the audio tape recorder; the primary differences are in the mechanical considerations of speed and size—one hour of audio recording requires a 2250-foot reel, while a 3000-foot reel is needed for a video recording of one hour's duration.

FILM AND SLIDE PROJECTION

While the video tape recording has become standard as a means of retaining video program material produced by means of the electronic camera, the television station still relies on movie film and slides. In addition to the entertaining movies, films also provide a means of bringing news events to the television audience. Where animation or movement is not desired, e.g., in station identification, commercials, public-service announcements, etc., slides are very convenient. Such slides are 35×27-mm color transparencies mounted in cardboard and arranged in trays for push-button changing in the control room; that is, pushing a button will take one slide from the projector and set in another one.

These projectors, in a separate room, are commonly arranged with mirrors or prisms (*optical multiplexer*) to project directly into the lens of a camera. Fig. 3-10 shows the two film projectors and one slide projector arranged to excite the single television camera. This arrangement is probably the most convenient and versatile. Complete control of this projecting unit, including the intensity of each projector lamp, permitting the fading in or out of each projector, is accomplished at the control console.

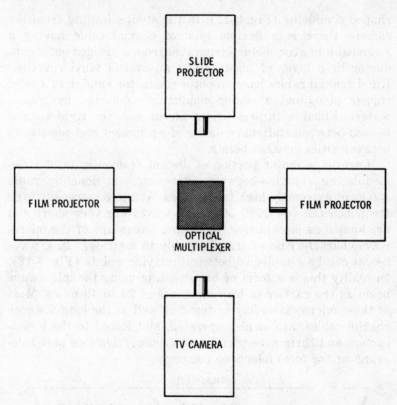

Fig. 3-10. Relative positions of slide and film projectors and camera.

LINES AND MICROWAVE RELAYS

Because of the wide frequency range (4.5 MHz) of the video modulating signal, the inductances, capacitances, and resistances of normal wires or telephone cables become excessive; that is, much of a video-signal wave would be lost within a common wire or telephone line of any appreciable length, and thus coaxial cables or microwave radio relays must be used. Coaxial cables have a conductor centered within an outer tube-

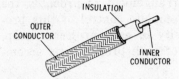

OUTER CONDUCTOR
INSULATION
INNER CONDUCTOR

Fig. 3-11. Construction of coaxial cable.

shaped conductor (Fig. 3-11). In the studio, leading from the camera there is a flexible type of coaxial cable having a stranded inner conductor (separated from a braided outer conductor by a layer of plastic) and an overall vinyl covering. Rigid coaxial cables have an outer conductor similar to a solid copper pipe, and a center conductor supported by plastic wafers. Filled with pressurized air or gas, the rigid coaxial is used between stationary pieces of equipment and sometimes between cities or other points.

However, a major portion of distant transmission of video modulating signals—between cities, etc.—is done by radio waves of extremely high frequencies. At these extremely high frequencies, above 3000 MHz, the waves are very short and are known as *microwaves*. By taking advantage of the microwave characteristic of traveling only in a straight line, wave beams can be established between relaying points (Fig. 3-12). In reality this is a form of broadcasting using the microwave beam as the carrier to leap distances of 20 to 40 miles. Most of these microwave-relay systems, as well as the long-distance coaxial cables, are owned, operated, and leased to the broadcasters and their networks by American Telephone and Telegraph or the local telephone company.

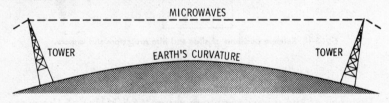

MICROWAVES

TOWER   EARTH'S CURVATURE   TOWER

Fig. 3-12. Microwave relay system.

AMPLIFIERS

Just like the audio current waves produced by microphones or phonograph pickups, the video current wave from the camera tube has a very small magnitude. To increase this magni-

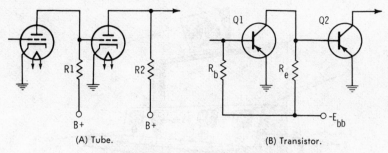

Fig. 3-13. Direct-coupled amplifier circuits.

tude requires the use of amplifier circuits. The wide range of frequencies found within the video current wave presents some difficulties. However, the video wave is not a true alternating wave—it does not change direction—but is a pulsating form of direct current. Therefore video wave amplifiers are often of the direct-coupled type, as shown by Fig. 3-13A, using electron tubes, and by Fig. 3-13B, using transistors. Video amplifiers are located within the camera to boost the signal to the control console and to power the camera's viewing screen. Other video amplifiers in the video studio console power other viewing screens, as well as boost the signal to the transmitter.

CONTROL CONSOLE

While the video control console serves the same purpose as the audio control console, it is considerably larger and will often require two or more operators. Fig. 3-14 shows a simplified video control console. Across the front of the console are four viewing screens (1) showing the pictures from the cameras, projectors, or networks. Push-button switches (2) beneath each of these viewing screens select the input to that position, while a vertical handle (2) adjusts a fader. At the center (3) other switches select the channel or channels to be passed on to the program line and the program monitor screen (4). Depending on the complexity of the program being produced, from two to four operators have a director seated at their backs to determine and state which channel is to be fed the program line. The director also instructs, through the use of headsets, the camera operators about the picture desired,

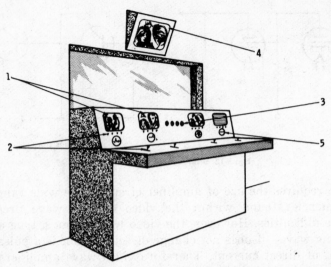

Fig. 3-14. Video studio console.

the brightness and contrast levels, the focus, etc. Small 3-inch oscilloscopes (5) displaying the waveform of each channel are located beneath or to the side of each viewing screen, providing a visual display of the scanning pulses. While a majority of the television stations depend on network programs and have just one studio and one control console, the larger stations may also have a master control console, with several subordinate consoles.

SYNCHRONIZATION SIGNAL GENERATORS

The timing center, the unit that keeps all of the operations of the television system in step, is the *synchronization signal generator*. Fig. 3-15 shows a simplified block diagram of this synchronization signal generator. A temperature-controlled crystal oscillator providing a harmonic or subharmonic of a 15,750-Hz signal is the heart of the generator. From this oscillator output, a fundamental of 15,750-Hz is derived to trigger the horizontal-pulse generator as well as to trigger a series of frequency multipliers and multivibrators to derive a 60-Hz signal. In addition to triggering the vertical-pulse generator, the 60-Hz signal is compared with that of the a-c power line to affect the reactance of an automatic frequency-control sys-

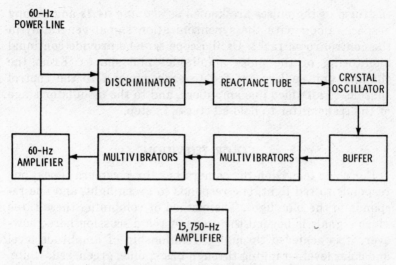

Fig. 3-15. Synchronizing signal generator.

tem. Thus, the outputs of the synchronization signal generator
are held in step with the frequency as well as the phase of the
a-c power supply. Then, with the receiver synchronizing system also held in step by that a-c power supply, the entire trans-
mission-reception process is stabilized.

Pulses developed by the synchronization signal generator
have a rounded or sawtooth form that will not hold the deflecting forces to a desirable level for a long enough time (Fig.
3-16A); that is, a sawtooth horizontal pulse might deflect the
beam only halfway across the screen, while a sawtooth horizontal pulse having an amplitude that stays above the desired
level for a long enough time will deflect the beam too quickly.
Accordingly, the sawtooth pulse must be clipped by limiting
action and its sides made steeper by frequency-selective additional clipping action (Fig. 3-16B). The circuits used to alter

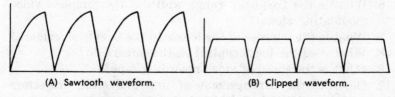

(A) Sawtooth waveform.   (B) Clipped waveform.

Fig. 3-16. Development of square synchronizing pulses.

39

the form of the pulses are known as *shaping units* and occupy a space, along with the synchronization signal generator, in the control-room racks. Oscilloscope screens provide continual monitoring of the pulse amplitudes and shapes. From the shaping unit, pulses are fed to each camera, to the control console, to all video line amplifiers, and to the modulator stage of the transmitter to hold all stages in step.

COLOR TELEVISION

For color television the camera has three camera tubes: one responds to red light, one responds to green light, and one responds to the blue light. The method of combining these three video signals is beyond the scope of the discussion here; however, it is achieved through a relationship of amplitude level and color level—ranging through black, blue, green, red, white, and all the various shades between. And while many of the factors of operations are more critical, the equipment and its basic principles are the same for color television as for black and white.

REVIEW QUESTIONS

1. How much light does a black object reflect? Does a blue object reflect as much light as a white object?
2. How do the silver salts on a photographic film react to white light?
3. Describe the electronic retina. Does a white-light ray cause the photosensitive globules to become positively or negatively charged?
4. What is scanning? What is the purpose of horizontal pulses? Of vertical pulses?
5. What is the number of frames per second? The number of lines per frame?
6. What is the frequency-range width of the complete video modulating signal?
7. What is the purpose of the lenses in the television camera?
8. What does the focus control on the camera do?
9. What is the speed of video-recording tape?
10. Describe the arrangement of film and slide projectors with respect to the television camera.

11. Why cannot telephone cables be used to carry the video modulating signals?
12. Who owns most of the microwave-relay systems?
13. What type of coupling is commonly used for video amplifiers?
14. What is the purpose of the small oscilloscope screens on the control console?
15. Why is it essential to compare the frequency and phase of the synchronization signal generator?
16. Does the synchronization signal generator produce a square pulse?

4

Carrier Origin

Although not as economically important now as in the past, the great Mississippi River, cutting through the heart of our country, has been an important carrier of freight. But a small stream rippling over the rocks far north in Minnesota is the origin of "Ole Man River." At the mouth, south of New Orleans, the amount of soil the river itself carries is almost unbelievable, while its boats and barges carry another great quantity of cargo. In broadcasting, the carrier also has a small beginning which is increased to a point of being capable of carrying the modulating signals. The small stream may carry as much in proportion as the mighty Mississippi, but its width and depth limit the load. A river must be wider than any boat it carries, and the broadcast carrier wave must have a sufficient width or frequency range.

CARRIER CHARACTERISTICS

Basically the carrier must be an alternating wave that can produce a sufficient standing wave to develop radiation (refer to Fig. 1-3). Carrier waves are radio-frequency or r-f waves and they range from 200,000 Hz upward. Amplitude-modula-

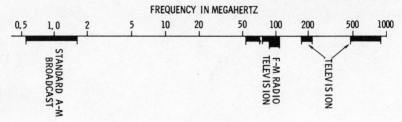

Fig. 4-1. Broadcast frequency spectrum.

tion radio broadcasting is concerned with the standard broadcasting range of 540 to 1600 kHz, the frequency-modulation range between 88 and 108 MHz, and the 82 television channels beginning at 54 MHz and extending to 890 MHz. Fig. 4-1 shows the relative position of these broadcast ranges on the frequency spectrum.

In reality the individual carrier wave has little or no frequency range, but the modulating signal adds to or otherwise alters the frequency. For example, when a carrier of 1,260,000 Hz (1260 kHz) is amplitude modulated by a 10,000-Hz audio signal, the resultant wave also contains a 1,270,000-Hz (1,260,-000 plus 10,000) wave. Thus in order to transmit audio signals having frequencies up to 5 kHz, each broadcast station bandwidth must be 10,000 Hz (10 kHz)—say from 1,260,000 to 1,270,000 Hz—for standard broadcast. However, the video modulating signal has a frequency spread of 4.5 MHz, and then, when the audio channel and other factors are added, the entire television channel has a width of 6 MHz. The frequency-modulation broadcast channels have a width of 0.2 MHz. For comparison, each television channel is 30 times as wide as an f-m channel, while each standard broadcast channel is only 0.05 times as wide as an f-m channel.

Other characteristics of the carrier wave include its amplitude and its waveform. The waveform is commonly considered to be a trigonometric sine wave, but its true form is important practically only if its harmonic content is excessive. A later chapter will deal with the amplitude of the carrier.

CRYSTAL OSCILLATORS

Origination of the carrier wave is assigned to a circuit known as the *oscillator*. Fundamentally an oscillator is an

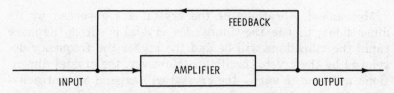

Fig. 4-2. Block diagram of basic oscillator.

amplifier circuit having a portion of its output fed back to its input (see Fig. 4-2). In broadcasting, where the frequency must be maintained to within a close tolerance, the crystal oscillator is used exclusively (Fig. 4-3). The inherent capacitance between the control grid and the anode serves as the feedback path. A pulse of anode current acts through the grid-anode capacitance to strike the thin slice of quartz crystal along its electrical axis. Mechanical vibrations result when the crystal is struck by an electrical pulse. These mechanical vibrations have a frequency depending on the crystal's dimensions and in turn develop electrical variations having the same frequency.

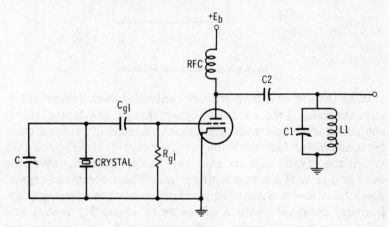

Fig. 4-3. Crystal oscillator circuit.

Acting about the more or less fixed value of grid-bias voltage, these electrical variations of the crystal swing the grid voltage to a value permitting a pulse of anode current to flow. These anode current pulses are accurately timed by the crystal frequency, the resulting resonant current circulating within the parallel circuit of L1 and C1. Fig. 4-4 shows a similar transistor oscillator circuit.

Mechanical vibrations of the crystal are governed by its dimensions; that is, the thinner the crystal is sliced, the more rapid the vibrations will be and the higher the frequency developed by the crystal oscillator. However, the crystal dimensions will tend to vary—the crystal will expand or contract—with changes of temperature, so the frequency also tends to vary. Various methods of cutting and grinding the crystal have been used to reduce the variations of frequency caused by changes of temperature. For the tolerance allowable for broad-

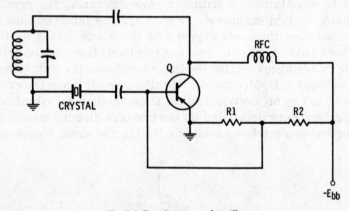

Fig. 4-4. Transistor crystal oscillator.

casting the use of a temperature-controlled oven (chamber) is advantageous. Like so many other things, the temperature-controlled oven has undergone much refinement; from a cumbersome metal box with one or two layers of asbestos into which the crystal and its case and holder were mounted, the oven and crystal are now a single unit. These combined crystal assemblies and constant-temperature ovens are commonly cylindrical in shape, with a diameter of about 2¼ inches and height of about 2½ inches, with prongs to fit the five-pronged tube socket and maybe a cap-type terminal on the side or top of the assembly. Internally the temperature is held at 75°C by a thermostat and electrical heating element, as indicated by an external thermometer (see Fig. 4-5). Along with the thermometer, a pilot light is usually provided to show that the heater is functioning. To provide for the possibility of a crystal-unit failure, the oscillator section has two such units with a switching arrangement. When these temperature-controlled

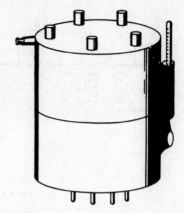

Fig. 4-5. Constant-temperature crystal oven.

units are operating properly, the temperature variation will be less than 2°C and the frequency deviation is commonly less than 5 Hz for standard broadcast channels or 500 Hz for frequency-modulation channels.

BUFFER STAGES

Following the oscillator are the *buffer stages*. The dictionary defines buffer as being anything that lessens or softens a shock. Just as fine china or glassware is packed in excelsior to prevent its breakage, it is necessary to cushion the oscillator against circuit factors that might alter its operations. The load of the oscillator is inductively coupled to its anode tank circuit, L1 and C1, by means of L2 of Fig. 4-6. If the load reflected into the oscillator tank circuit is large, the pulses fed back into the grid circuit may become too small to sustain oscillations. The load can also affect the resonant frequency of L1 and C1; this also limits the amplitude of the oscillations and those fed back to the grid circuit. Fig. 4-7 is the basic circuit of the buffer—a tuned r-f amplifier having a very low amplification.

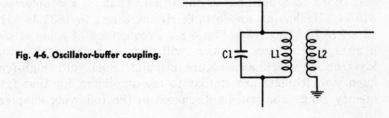

Fig. 4-6. Oscillator-buffer coupling.

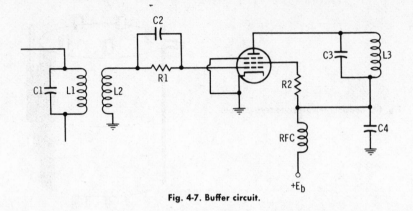

Fig. 4-7. Buffer circuit.

To avoid the possibility of oscillations starting within the buffer, and to keep the amplification small, a pentode tube with a low g_m rating or a low-beta-factor transistor will be used.

FREQUENCY MULTIPLIERS

There are oscillator circuits, Barkhausen-Kurz and klystron, which will develop the very high and the ultrahigh frequencies required for the frequency-modulation and television channels, but their stability is not adequate. Crystals having resonant or mode frequencies up to 100 MHz are available, but their stability and reliability are questionable above 5 or 10 MHz. For this reason, lower-frequency crystal oscillators are used with frequency multipliers. For example, one f-m transmitter manufacturer uses five multiplier stages—a doubler, a tripler, a tripler, a tripler, and a doubler—to give a total frequency multiplication of 108. Thus a crystal frequency of 815.74 kHz, which is readily available, will give a carrier frequency of 88.1 MHz (815.74 kHz × 108). Most multiplier circuits are similar to the tuned-plate tuned-grid buffer or amplifier, with a grid-biasing voltage of two or three times cutoff and an anode circuit tuned to a multiple of the input. That is, a doubler for 815.74 kHz has an anode tank circuit tuned to 1631.48 kHz (2 × 815.74 kHz). (See Fig. 4-8.) Frequencies of some of the ultrahigh television channels will require multipliers using klystron or Barkhausen-Kurz circuits. Such ultrahigh-frequency multipliers are similar to the amplifiers for that frequency range and will be discussed in the following chapter.

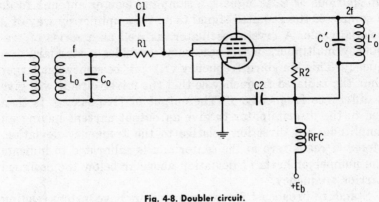

Fig. 4-8. Doubler circuit.

Multipliers, along with the oscillator and buffer stages, are usually housed within the transmitter cabinet.

FREQUENCY METERS

Since the broadcaster is required to have a continuous record of any frequency deviations, a *frequency meter* is needed. That is, the Federal Communications Commission requires that the frequency deviation be read from an approved frequency meter and recorded on the station log every 30 minutes. Fig. 4-9 shows the block diagram of a frequency meter. Located at some point remote enough from the transmitter not to pick

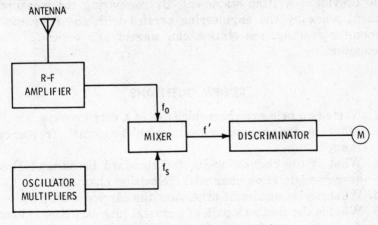

Fig. 4-9. Block diagram of frequency monitor.

up spurious or false signals, a sampling loop or antenna feeds a sample of the radiated signal to an r-f amplifier by way of a coaxial cable. A crystal oscillator, as well as a series of frequency multipliers when necessary, provides a standard frequency. This standard frequency (f_s) will be somewhat larger than the radiated frequency so that the mixer circuit will give a difference frequency, f'. The output of frequency f' is then fed to the discriminator to give an output current having an amplitude and direction relative to the frequency deviation. Meter M reads zero at the center and is calibrated to indicate the number of hertz of deviation above or below the assigned carrier frequency.

Standard-broadcast frequency monitors have meters reading 30-0-30 with 1-Hz divisions, while the monitors for frequency-modulation stations can be read to within 100-Hz deviation over a range from 3000 Hz above to 3000 Hz below the assigned carrier frequency. Of course, to maintain standard frequency f_s at its greatest stability, the crystal must be kept at a constant temperature within a temperature-controlled unit. Thus, the frequency monitor also has a heat-indicator light and thermometer.

As a further check and to correct any error that may occur within the frequency monitor, measurements are regularly made by an engineering service. The engineering service, located at a distance from the station, is paid to make a regular—usually monthly—measurement of the frequency deviation and to provide a written statement. By comparing the measurement made by the engineering service with the frequency-monitor reading, the station can correct any errors in the monitor.

REVIEW QUESTIONS

1. Name two primary characteristics of a carrier wave.
2. What is the frequency-modulation broadcast frequency range?
3. What is the channel width for standard broadcast? Frequency-modulation channels? Television channels?
4. What device or circuit originates the carrier wave?
5. What is the feedback path of a crystal tube oscillator? What determines the frequency of a quartz crystal?

6. Why is it necessary to keep the crystal at a fixed temperature? At what temperature is the crystal normally?
7. What follows the oscillator? What is a buffer stage?
8. What is a frequency multiplier? If the crystal frequency is 908.33 kHz and the total frequency multiplication is 108, what is the carrier frequency?
9. Why is a frequency meter required? Name at least four sections of the frequency meter. Is the frequency-meter crystal temperature controlled? Where is the zero reading on the frequency meter?

5

Carrier Amplification

The little boy enjoys imitating his father or older brother in hauling rocks or sand in his toy truck or wagon. But both the boy and the truck must grow before the resultant can be very impressive. Of course, the boy's mother may be very "impressed" with the amount of dirt he manages to carry within his clothes. Thus, the impression is really a combination of the amount carried and the situation. In the transmission, or broadcasting, of intelligence the result or impression is also a combination of the amount carried and the situation. Since the frequency range of the voice is narrow and the ears are commonly accustomed to knowing what may be said, the amount to be carried for voice communication is small. Therefore, the carrier for voice communication can also be small. For example, the amateur-radio operator with a carrier power of 50 watts or less often logs communications with all parts of the world. However, the commercial broadcasting is competing for listeners or viewers, and his product—the sound or the picture—must be acceptable. Listeners will not strain their ears to learn that brand A is better than brand X or to distinguish Beethoven from rock-and-roll.

PRIMARY SERVICE AREA

Advertisers are primarily interested in the number of people that can be reached by the advertising medium. That is, an advertising medium that reaches 100,000 people gives the advertiser twice as many prospective customers as the medium that reaches only 50,000 people. Accordingly, the primary service area of a broadcast station can be defined as that area being adequately served with entertainment, news, and information. With the listener attracted, the broadcast becomes an equally attractive advertising medium. To adequately excite the average standard broadcast receiver, the transmitter must have a sufficient amount of voltage induced into its antenna. This induced antenna voltage is expressed by the units of millivolts or microvolts per meter, indicating the electromotive force induced into a conductor having a length of one meter. However, many electrical devices—motors, neon signs, automobile ignitions, etc.—will also induce voltages into the antenna, causing noise or interference. The primary service area has a carrier-to-noise voltage ratio of at least 8 to 1. Accordingly, in business or factory areas, where interference can be expected to be greatest, the induced voltage must be at least 50 millivolts per meter, while in rural areas the field strength can be as much as 100 times less. Roughly, the field strength, E, is proportional to the square root of the radiated power P and indirectly proportional to the distance d:

$$E = \frac{186.4 \sqrt{PA}}{d}$$

where,

P is the radiated power in kilowatts,
d is the distance between the transmitter and receiver antenna in miles,
A is a complex factor relating frequency, the dielectric constant and conductivity of the earth, and actual distance,
E is the field strength in millivolts per meter.

Fig. 5-1 indicates graphically the variation of field strength with radiated power and distance, assuming the factor A to be

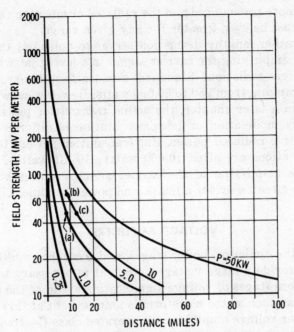

Fig. 5-1. Variation of field strength with distance.

1. While the doubling of the power P from 5 kilowatts to 10 kilowatts, as shown at points (a) and (b), increases the field strength from 50 to 70.7 millivolts per meter at 8.3 miles, the distance to the 50-millivolt-per-meter point would be extended to only about 11.8 miles (c) with the same increase in power. Although these are only approximate figures, they indicate that while the power must be sufficient to provide adequate service, there may be a limit to the practicality of increasing power.

In a little more practical vein, a power of 1 kilowatt with a frequency of 1000 kHz (center of standard broadcast range) will develop a field strength of about 0.5 millivolt per meter with soil having good conductivity, or about 0.04 millivolt per meter with poor-conductivity soil, at 50 miles. Moist loam like that found in the upper Mississippi, Ohio, and Missouri River valleys has fair to good conductivity, while the sandy soils that lose moisture rapidly in the southeastern and southwestern parts of the United States are poor in conductivity.

At the higher frequencies of frequency-modulation and television broadcasting, the attenuation and interference factors become more pronounced and the radiated or effective radiated power must be even greater for any given range.

This rather lengthy discussion serves to point out the necessity of amplifying the carrier signal to a level that will give the desired radiation. Standard broadcast stations radiate powers ranging from 250 to 50,000 watts. However, as we shall discuss in a later chapter, the actual transmitter power of a frequency modulation or television station is different from the effective radiated power. But transmitter powers for f-m and tv stations are often 10,000 watts (10 kilowatts). Naturally, the amplifying of the carrier signal requires voltage-amplifier circuits, driver circuits, and power-amplifier circuits.

VOLTAGE AMPLIFIERS

Since the oscillator, buffer stages, and frequency multipliers do not provide a large voltage output, it is necessary to have one or more stages of voltage amplification ahead of the power stage. Inasmuch as the waveform is unimportant at this point, the carrier voltage amplifiers are operated class-C—frequency modulation is not altered by changes in the waveform.

Fig. 5-2 indicates the relative position of these carrier voltage-amplifier stages as well as the other stages of the transmitter, and Fig. 5-3 shows the basic circuit for such a carrier voltage amplifier. Inductively coupled to the previous stages, the grid is driven positive to draw current, charging capacitance C1 and developing a biasing voltage across resistance R1. When the signal voltage raises the grid voltage to above cutoff, there occurs a pulse of anode current to start and to maintain the flywheel action of the resonant circuit L_o' and C_o'. Resistance R2 serves to reduce the supply voltage to that desired for

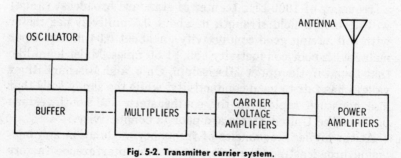

Fig. 5-2. Transmitter carrier system.

the screen grid, the pentode tube being used to lessen the possibility of undesired oscillations.

While it seems that transistors might be used in carrier voltage amplifiers, there would be very little advantage if the final power-output stage used tubes. That is, since tubes are required to develop powers above 100 watts, it would seem rather impractical to use transistors and tubes within the same unit. By the same reasoning, we can assume the stage preceding the final power-output stage—the driver—will be a voltage amplifier rather than the power amplifier required to drive a transistor output stage.

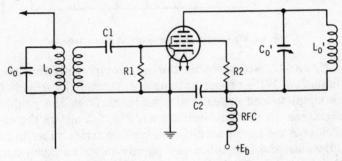

Fig. 5-3. Basic carrier voltage amplifier.

CARRIER POWER AMPLIFIER

The circuits for developing the power radiated from the transmitting-antenna system are dependent on the form of modulation and the frequency. Standard broadcast stations use amplitude modulation occurring within the final power-output stage. Since the amplitude of the carrier output must vary directly with the variations of the audio modulating wave, the power amplifier must have a linear characteristic. That is, the power-amplifier anode current must vary directly with the audio-modulating voltage. As the audio voltage reaches a maximum positive value, the carrier variation must likewise become maximum, while the minimum carrier variation must occur with the maximum negative value of audio voltage.

Such linearity is possible with class-A or class-B power amplifiers. As shown by the circuit of Fig. 5-4, the class-B r-f power amplifier is of the push-pull type and has the advantages of efficiency and reduction of undesirable harmonics. Capaci-

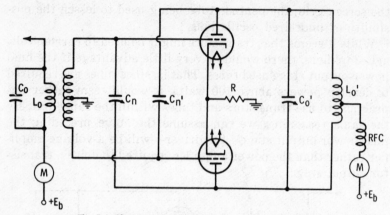

Fig. 5-4. Class-B push-pull carrier output power amplifier.

tors C_n and C_n' are probably the only components that require explanation. With proper adjustment, C_n and C_n' provide feedback equal to and opposite the feedback from the grid-anode capacitance, to prevent oscillations. Fig. 5-5 shows the circuit of a class-A r-f power amplifier using two triode tubes in parallel. Because the two tubes can supply twice as much current without excessive heat, the power (I^2R) developed is four times that from one tube. Power can be multiplied by 16 when four

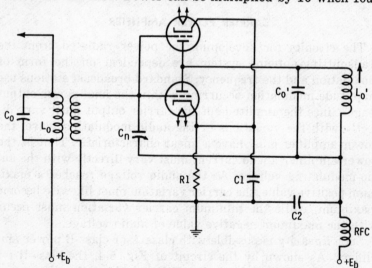

Fig. 5-5. Class-A carrier power amplifier circuit with triodes in parallel.

tubes are used in this parallel manner. With just one neutralizing capacitor, C_n, the class-A amplifier has the advantage of being simple.

The carrier power amplifier of the video transmitter is also an amplitude-modulated stage. However, because of the large amounts of power involved, the modulation will likely occur within the driver—the stage preceding the power amplifier. Thus, the driver would also have to be operated linear class A or class B.

Frequency modulation occurs in the oscillator stage, with following stages required only to follow the frequency variations. Frequency-modulation transmitters are often constructed in sections—an exciter section followed by a series of power-amplifier sections. The exciter section includes the oscillator, modulator, buffer stage, multipliers, and 100- or 250-watt power amplifier. Additional sections step up the power to 1000 and 10,000 watts. Each section has its own rectifying power supply. Since the amplitude of the frequency-modulated carrier stays at a steady value and only the frequency varies, the power amplifier can be operated class C.

TUNING

Observation of the carrier voltage and power amplifier circuits shown above will indicate that either the inductance or the capacitance, or both, of the resonant tank circuits is variable. Most of these variable components will be stable enough not to need adjustment after the initial alignment, but those related to the carrier power amplifier are more critical and more likely to change.

In modern transmitters these variable components of the carrier power amplifier are adjusted by means of electric motors and gears. One knob on the front panel of the transmitter selects the motor and the circuit to be tuned, while a second knob, a switch spring-loaded to always return to the center off-position, selects the direction of the motor as well as turning it on and off. Tuning is accomplished by manipulating this motor-switch knob until a minimum of d-c current is indicated by the meter of the circuit being tuned. That is, the d-c component of the anode current will be minimum when the resonant tank circuit is precisely tuned to the carrier frequency.

While the resonant tank circuits of amplifiers for the very high- and ultrahigh-frequency television transmitters replace the usual capacitors and inductors with resonant transmission lines or cavities, the tuning is accomplished in much the same manner. Fig. 5-6 shows the motor-driven tuning mechanism of a resonant transmission line.

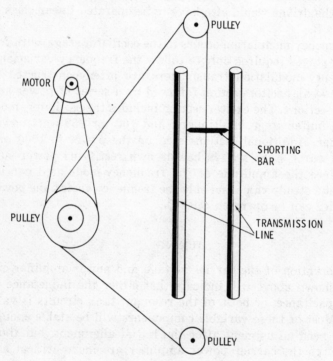

Fig. 5-6. Motor-driven tuning of resonant transmission line.

METERS

Just as with other parts of the broadcasting system, the carrier power amplifier must have indicators of its basic parameters—its anode current, anode voltage, and filament voltage. The Federal Communications Commission requires that the anode voltage and current of the carrier power amplifier be read and recorded every 30 minutes. That record, the log, must also show the output and/or antenna current or its relative value. So the front panel of the transmitter will have at least the three meters—anode voltage, anode current, and output current. Often the anode-current meter is arranged with a switch to indicate the current of other circuits. Each meter has a range equal to nearly double its normal reading; that is, the normal reading will be near the center of the meter scale. The output and antenna meters will be discussed further in the chapters on transmission lines and antennas.

HEAT ELIMINATION

The search is still on for perpetual motion, but as yet all machines and devices known to man consume or take in more power than they put out. Shove this book across the table and note that it does not perpetually slide. Friction soon overcomes the initial pulse of power. In electronics, and more specifically in the carrier power amplifier, the friction results in heat. This heat represents lost power and is often equal to the output power. So if the output power is 10,000 watts, there may also be 10,000 watts, or about 570 Btu per minute, of heat developed. By comparison, 100,000 Btu per hour or 1666 Btu per minute will adequately heat the average home. Thus, the heat loss from

Courtesy General Electric Co.

Fig. 5-7. Power amplifier tube with heat-radiating fins.

a 10,000-watt transmitter can very often heat the small room in which the transmitter is housed, but such heat can be an equal disadvantage during the warm seasons. Moreover, unless the heat is carried away, the transmitter and its components may be damaged.

In years past, the circulation of distilled water over the exposed surface of the tube anode served to carry away the heat. However, in modern transmitters, heat-radiating fins (Fig. 5-7) exposed to circulating air dissipate the heat. In the transmitter cabinet(s), blowers in their lower sections pull cool air in through *Fiberglas* filters and out to overhead ducts. Provision is made to channel these ducts to the outside or to the inside.

REVIEW QUESTIONS

1. Define the primary service area. What is the desirable carrier-to-noise voltage ratio within the primary service area?
2. If the radiated power is increased from 250 to 1000 watts, what is the increase in field strength at a given distance?
3. What is the class of operation for carrier voltage amplifiers?
4. Why are pentode tubes used for carrier voltage amplifiers?
5. Why are carrier power amplifiers operated as class A or class B for amplitude modulation?
6. What is the purpose of capacitors C_n and C_n' in Fig. 5-4?
7. What stages are included within the exciter section of a frequency-modulation transmitter?
8. Are the resonant tank circuits of the carrier power amplifiers tuned by direct manual means?
9. Name the three meters required by FCC regulations.
10. What is the result of friction in electronic equipment? Why do some power-amplifier tubes have radiating fins?

6

Amplitude Modulation

In the previous chapters the various loads or modulating signals and carriers were discussed. Now, with the two signals developed, the problem is to load or to modulate the modulating signal into or onto the carrier. Comparing the carrier signal with a long train of flatcars, its silhouette is very even. If a load is piled onto these flatcars, the silhouette will have a varying height. However, if the load is in some manner worked into the flatcars so they vary in spacing and length, that silhouette will still appear even. Thus, the load or modulating signal can be loaded onto the carrier to alter its amplitude. This process is called *amplitude modulation*.

AMPLITUDE MODULATOR

Fig. 6-1 shows a basic circuit for the amplitude modulating of a carrier signal. The modulator portion of the circuit is an audio power amplifier which varies the carrier-amplifier supply voltage. The audio-frequency signal develops an alternating magnetic field within transformer T1 to produce a voltage between points A and B. As point A becomes positive with respect

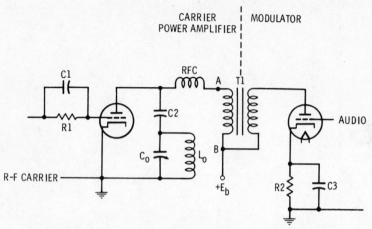

Fig. 6-1. Basic circuit for amplitude modulating a carrier signal.

to point B, the anode of the carrier amplifier becomes more positive and attracts a greater number of electrons. Conversely, on the other half of the audio cycle, the anode becomes less positive to attract fewer electrons. So the audio- or video-signal voltage, produced by the modulator portion in Fig. 6-1, causes the carrier signal to vary in amplitude.

The limit of such amplitude modulation is reached when the audio or video signal has a peak value equal to the anode supply voltage. Negative peak audio- or video-signal values equal to the anode supply voltage reduce the carrier signal to a trough value of zero as a limit; see Fig. 6-2 (the trough value is the minimum value of the modulated wave).

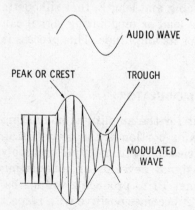

Fig. 6-2. Waveform of modulated carrier signal.

MODULATION PERCENTAGE

The *modulation factor*, *m*, of an a-m wave is the ratio of half the difference between the maximum and minimum amplitudes to the amplitude of the unmodulated carrier. The *modulation percentage* of an a-m wave is the modulation factor multiplied by 100. Fig. 6-3 may provide a better understanding of modulation percentage, *M*, as being the 100 times the ratio of the difference between the modulated wave's peak and trough values, *H* and *K*, to two times the unmodulated wave's amplitude, *C*:

$$M = \frac{(H - K)}{2C} \times 100$$

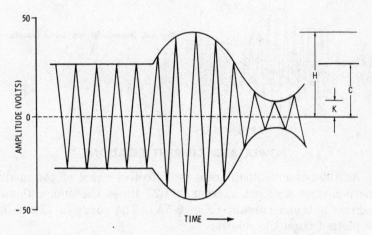

Fig. 6-3. Factors in calculating modulation percentage.

As an example, the modulation percentage will be 60 when the unmodulated amplitude is 25 volts, trough value *K* is 10 volts, and the peak value is 40 volts:

$$\frac{(40 - 10)}{2 \times 25} \times 100 = 60$$

One-hundred-percent modulation occurs when the trough value, *K*, becomes zero and the peak value, *H*, is equal to twice the unmodulated amplitude, *C*; that is, if *C* equals 25 volts and *H* equals 50 volts, when *K* is zero the modulation is 100 percent. Overmodulation, producing distortion, results when the negative half-cycle of the audio or video signal swings beyond the anode-current cutoff limit (Fig. 6-4). The result of this overmodulation is similar to clipping of the negative half of the audio cycle, giving a more or less square waveform with many undesirable harmonics. But since the radiated power is increased as the modulation is increased, the modulation percentage must be kept at a fairly high level: 85 to 95 percent on the louder passages of sound or on the synchronizing pulses of the video signal.

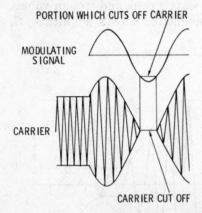

Fig. 6-4. Overmodulated carrier waveform.

POWER AND CURRENT RELATIONS

At 100-percent modulation the effective value of the modulated-carrier antenna current is 1.23 times the unmodulated-carrier antenna current (Fig. 6-5A). The curve in Fig. 6-5A is plotted from the relation

$$I_m = I_u \sqrt{1 + \frac{m^2}{2}} \qquad \text{or} \qquad \frac{I_m}{I_u} = \sqrt{1 + \frac{m^2}{2}}$$

where,

I_m is the modulated-carrier antenna current,
I_u is the unmodulated-carrier antenna current,
m is the modulation factor.

Since the output power varies as the square of the antenna current, it may be written as

$$P_m = P_u \left(1 + \frac{m^2}{2}\right) \qquad \text{or} \qquad \frac{P_m}{P_u} = 1 + \frac{m^2}{2}$$

where,

P_m is the modulated-carrier output power,
P_u is the unmodulated-carrier output power,
m is the modulation factor.

The ratio $P_m:P_u$ is plotted in Fig. 6-5B as a function of the modulation percentage, M ($=100m$). Thus, at 100-percent modulation, the modulated-carrier output power is $(1.23)^2 = 1.5$ times the unmodulated-carrier output power.

One-hundred-percent modulation increases the power output to 1.5 of the output without modulation. The carrier power amplifier supplies only 1.0 of the output, while the modulator must

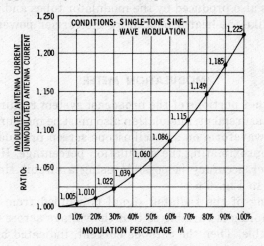

(A) Relative antenna current.

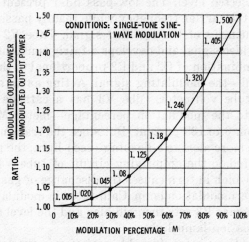

(B) Relative output power.

Fig. 6-5. Variation of carrier current and power with modulation percentage.

supply the additional 0.5 of the output for 100-percent modulation. Accordingly, to modulate a 1000-watt carrier, the modulator must provide 500 watts. Thus the modulator, contrary to that shown by Fig. 6-1, is often a class-B push-pull amplifier using large tubes similar to those of the carrier power amplifier. With the greater carrier power, up to 50,000 watts, it is often necessary to use a number of tubes in parallel and push-pull. Heat is also produced by the modulator tubes and must be exhausted, like the heat produced by the carrier power-amplifier tubes.

MODULATION METER

Just as other portions of the broadcast system require visual forms of measurement, modulation also must be measured. Display of the waveform on an oscilloscope screen provides a fair means of approximating the modulation percentage. However, much greater accuracy is possible using a circuit similar to that shown in Fig. 6-6.

A sampling of the radiated signal is coupled from L1 into L2; this coupling is variable so that the voltage across tube V1 is also variable. Then the cathode current, indicated by meter M1 and representative of the carrier amplitude, can be adjusted to a selected level. The low-pass filter presents a high impedance to the carrier frequency while readily passing audio or video frequencies of the rectified signal. Tube V2 rectifies the audio or video signal and develops a fairly constant voltage across the combination of C2 and R2 proportional to that audio or video signal—the modulating signal. Acting as an amplifier and vacuum-tube voltmeter, tube V3 has a cathode current proportional to the modulation percentage—meter M2 being calibrated from 0 to 133 percent. But since the transmitter engineer will be more alert to a flashing (red) light, the modulating signal is fed to the amplifying circuit of tube V4, biased below cutoff, which in turn causes the discharge of gas tube V5 to light the overmodulation lamp. Calibrated in modulation percentage, resistance R3 sets the grid bias and the level at which the overmodulation lamp lights.

In operation there is considerable variation in the recurrence and duration of the overmodulation lamp lighting. Some engineers prefer to set the modulation percent low and allow the lamp to light frequently. Other engineers prefer to set the modulation percent higher and allow the lamp to light rarely. (We wonder if a dual-lamp system, amber and red, wouldn't be advantageous.) Care must be taken not to confuse the percentage scale of the vu meter and that of the modulation meter. Response of the modulation meter is much faster than that of the vu meter so that passages of modulating signal showing a fairly low level at the studio console may indicate a higher level at the transmitter.

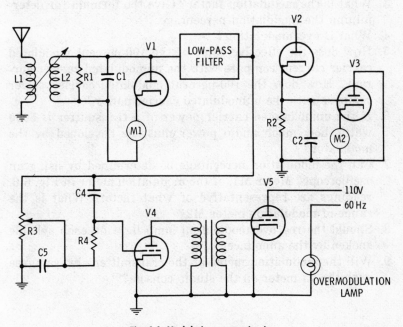

Fig. 6-6. Modulation meter circuit.

LIMITER AMPLIFIER

In conjunction with the modulator amplifier, a *limiter amplifier* is often used to reduce the possibility of overmodulation. By increasing the amplitude of the audio signal coming from the studio, the limiter amplifier also acts as a line amplifier. However, its primary function is guarding against high-level passages that would overmodulate the carrier, though it also tends to compress many of the high studio frequencies. While overmodulation is possible in television transmitters—also amplitude modulated—the high-level passages will be the synchronizing pulses which are already precisely controlled and shaped.

REVIEW QUESTIONS

1. What type of circuit is the amplitude modulator? Does this modulator cause changes within the grid circuit or within the anode circuit of the carrier power amplifier?
2. What is the limit of amplitude modulation?
3. What is the modulation factor? Give the formula for determining the modulation percentage.
4. What is overmodulation?
5. How does the effective value of the 100-percent modulated carrier current compare with the unmodulated carrier current? How does the 100-percent modulated carrier power compare with the unmodulated carrier power?
6. If the unmodulated carrier power of a transmitter is 5000 watts, how much audio power must be developed by the modulator?
7. Can the modulation percentage be determined by using an oscilloscope? Meter M1, of the modulation meter in Fig. 6-6, readings are representative of what factor? What is the range of modulation meter M2?
8. Should the red overmodulation lamp light on each syllable spoken by the announcer?
9. Will the modulation meter at the transmitter always agree with the vu meter on the studio console?

7

Frequency Modulation

Medical science has found means of injecting "food" directly into our bloodstream. While not as enjoyable as eating, "food" taken in this manner, even though it does not fill the stomach with bulk or volume, does accomplish the same goal. Similarly, frequency modulation delivers the desired audio signal to its goal without addition of bulk or amplitude.

FUNDAMENTAL CIRCUIT

Frequency modulation involves the change of frequency according to the amplitude of the audio signal. That is, the greater the amplitude of the audio signal, the greater will be the change or deviation of the carrier frequency. Frequency modulation is not used for video modulating signals, but it is used for the sound (audio) portion of television channels and for the f-m broadcasting channels, from 88 to 108 MHz.

Fig. 7-1 shows a Hartley oscillator with a capacitor microphone in parallel with the resonant tuned circuit. Sound waves

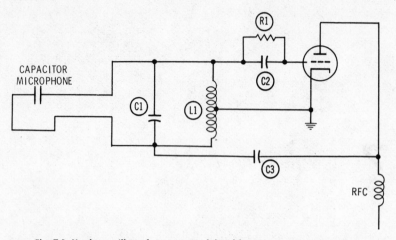

Fig. 7-1. Hartley oscillator frequency modulated by capacitor-type microphone.

striking the diaphragm of this capacitor microphone alter its capacitance and the resonant frequency. Another circuit (Fig. 7-2) adds inductance or capacitance by means of switches S1 and S2. When switch S1 is closed, the oscillator frequency is decreased, as shown between B and C of Fig. 7-3. Opening switch S1 at point C brings the frequency back to normal. In-

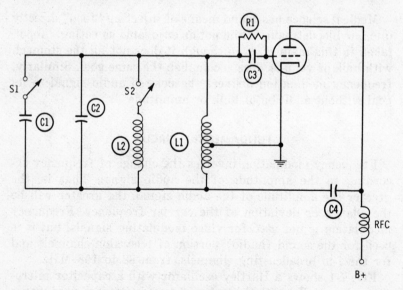

Fig. 7-2. Frequency-modulated Hartley oscillator.

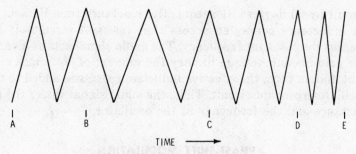

Fig. 7-3. Frequency-modulated waveform.

ductance L2 is placed in parallel with the resonant circuit when switch S2 is closed, thus increasing the oscillator frequency between D and E of Fig. 7-3. Thus, the waveform of Fig. 7-3 has been frequency modulated.

REACTANCE-TUBE MODULATION

Fig. 7-4 is a simplified schematic of a reactance-tube frequency modulator. V1 is the reactance tube, and V2 is the oscillator. The anode, or plate, of V1 is coupled to the oscillators resonant circuit through capacitor C5. Capacitor C2 feeds r-f signals to a phase-splitting network consisting of R2 and C_s. R2 is chosen so that the reactance of C_s, the input and stray capacitances of reactance tube V1, is negligible in comparison. The r-f current is almost in phase with the r-f voltage across R2 and C_s, while the r-f voltage across C_s lags that across the oscillator tuned circuit by almost 90 degrees. Because this r-f voltage across C_s is also the voltage on the grid of V1, the anode current of V1 lags the voltage across the oscillator resonant

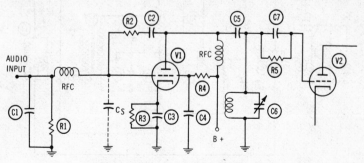

Fig. 7-4. Reactance-tube modulator circuit.

circuit by 90 degrees. Consequently, reactance tube V1 acts as an inductance connected across that resonant circuit—it increases the resonant frequency. The audio signal acts as a varying grid-biasing voltage to vary the amount of V1 anode current and, in turn, the effective inductive reactance added to the oscillator resonant circuit. Thus, the audio signal varies the inductance and the frequency of the oscillator.

PHASE-SHIFT MODULATION

Closely related to frequency modulation is another form known as *phase modulation*. Phase modulation, or phase shifting, alters the time relationships of the carrier wave in relation to the audio modulating frequency and amplitude. Alteration of the time and phase relations also produces frequency deviations, as shown by Fig. 7-3. Fig. 7-5 shows a simple phase-shift modulation circuit. The r-f voltage from the crystal oscillator, fed to the grid of tube V1, leads the oscillator anode voltage by 45 degrees because of the phase-shifting action of R3-L2. Combination R2-C3 causes the voltage applied to the grid of V2 to lag that of the oscillator anode by 45 degrees. Under normal operating conditions the anode currents are of the same amplitude and of equal but opposite phase to produce a combined current that is in phase with that of the oscillator anode. However, the audio modulating signal fed into the cathodes of V1

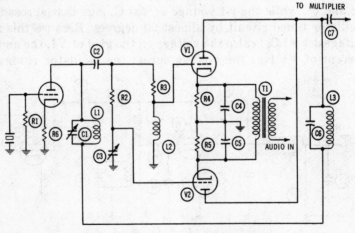

Fig. 7-5. A simple phase-modulation circuit.

and V2 by way of transformer T1 alternately increases or decreases the two out-of-phase currents. Thus the amount of phase shift, lead or lag, depends on the amplitude of the audio modulating signal. Frequency deviation F_d is then the product of the phase shift or deviation, θ_d, times the audio-signal or modulating frequency, f:

$$F_d = \theta_d f$$

where,

F_d and f are measured in hertz,
θ_d is measured in radians.

PHASITRON MODULATION

While the reactance tube and the phase-shift circuits discussed above provide means for frequency modulating, some of their characteristics leave much to be desired. Therefore, most f-m transmitters used for commercial broadcasting are modulated by a special electron tube—the phasitron—and its related circuit. The heart of the phasitron is a cathode, electrostatic-focus, and three-phase deflection system producing a sheet of electrons shaped like a disc having a rippled surface (see Fig. 7-6). Remember that this is an abstract disc of the negatively charged electrons. Then the three-phase variation of electrostatic forces moves around the axis so that the electron

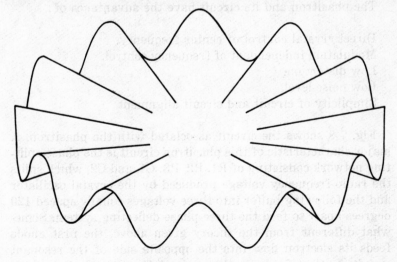

Fig. 7-6. Electron disc in phasitron tube.

disc and its ripples seem to rotate about the cathode at the center of the tube. At the outer edge of this electron disc is a positively charged anode having 12 rectangular holes above and 12 rectangular holes below the plane of the disc.

Beyond this first anode, a second anode attracts those electrons striking the holes of the first anode (see Fig. 7-7). The quantity of electrons reaching the second anode varies as the electron disc rotates with a frequency equal to that of the crystal oscillator. But the passage of an audio-signal current

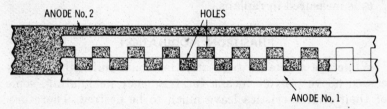

Fig. 7-7. First and second anodes in phasitron tube.

through a magnetic coil surrounding the tube produces an angular displacement of the electron disc and a phase shift in the electron flow or current to the second anode. Therefore, the output current from the second anode is phase modulated and, in turn, frequency modulated as with the phase-shift modulator above.

The phasitron and its circuit have the advantages of:

Direct crystal control of center frequency.
Modulation independent of frequency control.
Low distortion.
Low noise level.
Simplicity of circuit and circuit alignment.

Fig. 7-8 shows the circuit associated with the phasitron. A major characteristic of this phasitron circuit is the phase-splitting network consisting of R1, R2, R3, C1, and C2, which splits the radio-frequency voltage produced by the crystal oscillator and the following buffer into three voltages equally spaced 120 degrees apart to feed the three-phase deflecting system. Somewhat different from the theory given above, the first anode feeds its electron flow into the opposite side of the resonant circuit, L_0-C_0. Of course, this current from the first anode is essentially 180 degrees out of phase with that of the second anode to properly feed opposite sides of the resonant circuit. Coil L3 is the magnetic coil surrounding the tube. Other features of the phasitron circuit are fairly self-explanatory.

When the magnetic coil receives an audio-frequency power of 50 milliwatts and the crystal oscillator delivers a 220-kHz signal, the phasitron will produce a deviation of 175 Hz. Frequency multiplication of 432 then will increase the output carrier frequency to 95.04 MHz (220 kHz × 432) and the frequency deviation to 75.6 kHz (175 Hz × 432).

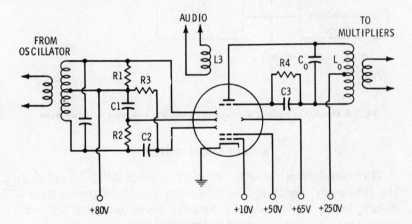

Fig. 7-8. Phasitron circuit.

MODULATION PERCENTAGE

The modulation percentage for frequency modulation is 100 times the ratio of the frequency deviation to the allowable frequency deviation. For example, f-m broadcast stations (88 to 108 MHz) are allowed a modulating deviation of 75,000 Hz from the carrier center frequency; this is taken to be 100-percent modulation:

$$M = \frac{\Delta f}{\Delta f_o} \times 100$$

where,
    M is the modulation percentage,
    Δf is the actual frequency deviation,
    Δf_o is the allowable frequency deviation.

A deviation of 60,000 Hz for an f-m broadcast station corresponds to a modulation of 80 percent. Some types of f-m transmitters are allowed a modulating deviation of only 3000 Hz.

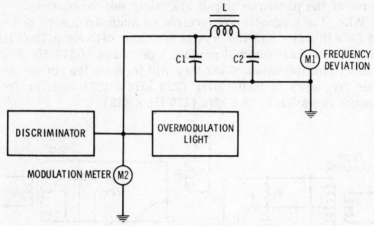

Fig. 7-9. Modulation meter, overmodulation light, and frequency-deviation meter.

MODULATION METER

The modulation meter for frequency modulation is added to the frequency monitor. The frequency monitor already uses a discriminator to detect any frequency deviations. Fig. 7-9 indicates that the output of the discriminator feeds directly to the modulation meter, reading from 0 to 133 percent. A filter, a series inductance with shunt capacitances, between the discriminator and the frequency meter blocks the audio-frequency deviations and passes only the direct-current component indicative of any carrier-frequency deviation.

As with the amplitude-modulation meter, an overmodulation (red) light is provided as a part of the frequency-modulation meter. The overmodulation-light circuit is the same as that for amplitude modulation. However, to compensate for the inadequacies of many f-m receivers, the overmodulation level is often set at a very low level, viz, 60 or 70 percent.

REVIEW QUESTIONS

1. What is frequency modulation?
2. Is frequency modulation used for video modulating signals?

3. Discuss the use of a capacitor microphone to frequency modulate an oscillator.
4. What effect does the reactance tube have on the resonant circuit?
5. What is phase modulation? Does phase modulation also produce frequency modulation?
6. Name the special electron tube used for frequency modulation. Is its ripple-surfaced disc made of metal? How is the audio modulating signal introduced into this special tube?
7. List three of the five advantages of the phasitron circuit.
8. When the allowable frequency deviation is 25,000 Hz and the actual frequency deviation is 22,000 Hz, what is the modulation percentage?
9. Why is the overmodulation level often set very low for f-m transmitters?

8

Power Supplies

The stagecoach had its relay station, the railroad's "iron horse" had its water tower and its wood or coal stop, and our automobile has the service station. In a like manner, our broadcast-station equipment must have a source of energy. Just as the hay fed to the horses, the coal or wood fed to the "iron-horse" locomotive, and the gasoline fed to our automobile are all foods fitted to the purpose, so must the energy supplied to the broadcast station be of proper form.

PRIMARY ENERGY SOURCE

Since the broadcast station and its apparatus are electrical in nature, the primary energy supplier will be the electric utility. Just as it does for other businesses and industries, the utility can supply the broadcaster with alternating current in single-phase or three-phase form. While some industries, foundries, and electroplaters, use power delivered at 2200 volts, the 220-volt level is normal for broadcast stations. That is, the effective value of the single-phase voltage is 220 volts, while a grounded center tap divides it as 110-0-110 volts (actual effective values are nearer 234 and 117 volts). Each phase of the three-phase voltage is rated at 220 volts.

As a matter of review, Fig. 8-1A indicates the variation of a single-phase voltage and current, and Fig. 8-1B shows the three voltage or current variations of the three-phase system. The three-phase system consists of three alternating voltages spaced or timed ⅓ cycle apart.

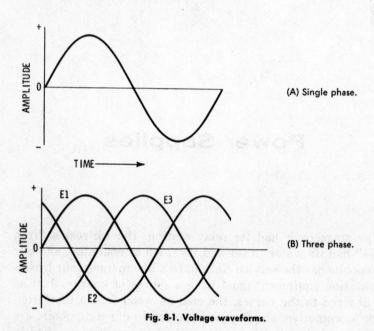

Fig. 8-1. Voltage waveforms.

Typically the power demand of a transmitter can be taken to be 20 to 30 times its output, with a power factor of about 90 percent. A rough estimate of this power demand can then be made with this equation:

$$\text{Power Demand} = \frac{30P_o}{0.9}$$

$$= 33\,P_o$$

where,

P_o is the output power of the transmitter.

Thus, a transmitter having an output of 1 kilowatt could be expected to have a power demand of 33 kilowatts (or more correctly, 33 kilovolt-amperes). When this power demand exceeds 1 kilovolt-ampere, use of three-phase power becomes necessary. At the audio studio, the power demand may not exceed 5 or 10 kva (kilovolt-amperes) and a single-phase system will usually suffice. Somewhat greater will be the power demand of the video studio; here the three-phase system is needed.

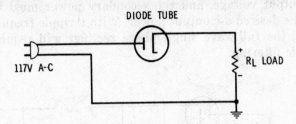

Fig. 8-2. Half-wave rectifier circuit.

RECTIFIER POWER SUPPLIES

Because the electron tubes or the transistors of all electronic and broadcasting equipment require direct current, rectifiers must be used to convert the alternating current. Rectifiers are devices that pass current readily in one direction and oppose current in the opposite direction. That is, when an alternating current is applied to a rectifier (the diode in Fig. 8-2), only half of the alternating-current wave is passed, as shown by Fig. 8-3A. However, both halves of the alternating-current wave

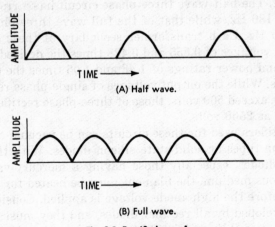

(A) Half wave.

(B) Full wave.

Fig. 8-3. Rectified waveforms.

will be passed in the same direction to load R_L in the circuit of Fig. 8-4. The full-wave rectifier of Fig. 8-4, with a filter consisting of inductor L1 and capacitors C1 and C2, will adequately provide the direct current for apparatus rated at less than 1 kilowatt. Each side of the secondary center tap of the transformer must have a voltage rating of 1.11 times the desired output voltage, and the secondary power must be 1.57 times the desired d-c output power. With a ripple frequency of 120 Hz, the full-wave single-phase rectifier will require considerable filtering.

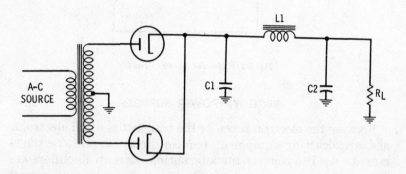

Fig. 8-4. Full-wave rectifier circuit.

Fig. 8-5 shows a half-wave and a full-wave three-phase rectifier circuit. The half-wave three-phase circuit has a ripple frequency of 180 Hz, while that of the full-wave three-phase circuit is 360 Hz. Each transformer secondary of these circuits must have voltages of 0.855 and 0.428 times the desired output voltages, and power ratings of 1.48 and 1.05 times the d-c output powers. While the output voltages of single-phase rectifiers will seldom exceed 500 volts, those of three-phase rectifiers may be as high as 2500 volts.

The rectifiers used for these circuits can be vacuum or gaseous electron tubes or solid-state silicon diodes. With the electron-tube diodes, especially those having a mercury-vapor or other gaseous medium, the filament must be heated for several minutes before the high anode voltage is applied. Considerable heat is developed by all rectifier diodes, and they must be well ventilated—possibly by using blowers.

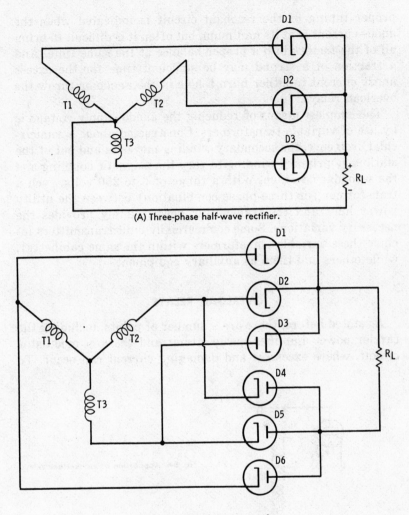

(A) Three-phase half-wave rectifier.

(B) Three-phase full-wave rectifier.

Fig. 8-5. Three-phase rectifier circuits.

VARIABLE TRANSFORMERS

Very often in tuning or otherwise adjusting the carrier power amplifier or its amplitude modulator, it is best to reduce the anode supply voltage. For example, in tuning the carrier power amplifier's resonant circuit, the anode current can become excessive and permanently damage the tubes. Of course, proper tuning of the resonant circuit is indicated when the anode current is at its minimum, but often it is difficult to bring all of the factors into a proper balance at the same time. And a fraction of a second may be sufficient time for the excess anode current to either burn a hole in the anode or throw the overload relays.

The simplest means of reducing the anode supply voltage is by use of variable transformers. Constructed about a semicircular iron core, the secondary winding moves in and out of the stationary primary winding to vary the magnetic coupling and the secondary voltage. With a range of 0 to 250 volts, such a transformer (or three-phase combination) between the utility power lines and the transmitter power supply provides the necessary variations. Some commercially built transmitters include these variable transformers within the same cabinet(s), while others add them as auxiliary equipment.

OVERLOAD RELAYS

As stated before, there are a number of points, including the carrier power-amplifier anode circuit and the a-m modulator circuit, where excessive and damaging current can occur. To

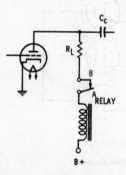

Fig. 8-6. Application of an overload relay.

eliminate the possibility of such excessive currents, overload relays are common in these circuits. Fig. 8-6 shows an application of a simple overload relay. When the current through the coil reaches a fixed level, a magnetic force is developed that pulls arm A down from contact B, opening the circuit. For more precise adjustment, overload relays for transmitters have a hydraulic cylinder instead of movable arm A of Fig. 8-6.

DOOR INTERLOCKS

The danger of electrical shock or even electrocution is present in most electronic equipment. Even the normal 117 volts of our household outlets can cause much pain in the form of a shock and, under proper conditions, death. So with voltages as high as 30,000 volts in broadcast apparatus, the danger becomes extreme. Therefore, many of the doors or covers of the transmitter and other broadcasting apparatus are equipped with interlock switches that cut off all power when the doors or covers are opened.

FILAMENT TRANSFORMERS

In contrast to many home radio and television receivers using a series connection of tube filaments—as one filament burns out, all other filaments cease to function—the filaments of broadcast apparatus are wired in parallel. By being wired in parallel, a burnt-out filament has no effect on others of the circuit and tube life is increased. To supply the low voltages (6.3 volts for the smaller tubes and 10 volts for the larger transmitter tubes) filament transformers are used. These filament transformers may also be preceded by a variable transformer.

REVIEW QUESTIONS

1. What is the primary energy supplier of the broadcast station? Describe the three-phase form of alternating current.
2. Estimate the power demand of a 5-kilowatt transmitter.
3. What is a rectifier? What is the ripple frequency of the full-wave single-phase rectifier with a 60-Hz source?
4. What is the ripple frequency of a half-wave three-phase rectifier with a 60-Hz source? Of a full-wave three-phase rectifier?
5. Should the anode voltage be applied to an electron-tube diode at the same time as the filament voltage?
6. Describe the construction of the variable transformer.
7. Why are overload relays used?
8. Why are interlock switches used?

9

Transmission Lines

People are often amazed to see how small the pin is that couples the giant freight trailer to its tractor. But this small coupling pin, along with the well-greased flat-surfaced bearing—the "fifth wheel"—adequately provides coupling of the tractor force to the trailer and its load. In broadcasting the transmitter develops the power and the force that must be coupled to the radiating elements or antenna. Since this coupling involves the movement of electrons—current—the coupling device must be some form of electrical conductor. At the carrier frequencies such conductors are known as *transmission lines*.

TRANSMISSION-LINE TYPES

There are basically three types of transmission lines used to carry the radio-frequency current from the transmitter to the antenna and its associated equipment. A very simple type, used exclusively in pioneer broadcasting, is the two-wire line consisting of two wires made parallel by carefully spaced insula-

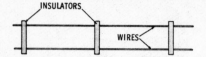

Fig. 9-1. Two-wire line.

tors (see Fig. 9-1). Held fairly parallel to the earth by vertical supports, the two-wire line is fairly nonradiating. The two-wire line is inexpensive and relatively simple to construct, but it is subject to having undesirable voltages induced. One advantage of the two-wire line is the variation of characteristic impedance for which the line may be designed—from about 200 to 800 ohms.

A second basic type of transmission line is the flexible coaxial cable for the smaller amounts of power: 250 watts or less. Coaxial cables (see Fig. 9-2) have a conductor centered within an outer tube-shaped conductor. Flexible coaxial cables have a stranded inner conductor separated from the braided outer conductor by a layer of plastic, with the entire cable covered by a vinyl jacket. A newer type uses a plastic foam between the inner and outer conductors. While it is possible to design coaxial cables with characteristic impedances as high as 200 ohms, the commercially available cables have impedances of 50, 52, 70, 72, 75, 90, etc. ohms.

Rigid coaxial cable has an outer conductor similar to a solid copper pipe, and a center conductor supported by perforated plastic wafers. To keep out moisture, the space between the inner and the outer conductors of rigid coaxial cables is kept filled with compressed dry air or gas. Dimensions of this rigid coaxial cable vary from that having a 1-inch diameter shipped in coils of 100-foot lengths, to 4-inch-diameter sections of 6-foot lengths. Naturally, the larger-sized coaxial cables, having more space between the inner and the outer conductors, require a greater amount of dry air or gas and electrically powered compressors. There is, however, evidence that when a high-powered transmitter is operated continuously, 24 hours

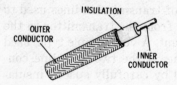

Fig. 9-2. Construction of coaxial cable.

a day, moisture does not develop within the cable and so it need not be pressurized with dry air or gas. While some installations have buried the coaxial cable underground, the majority support the cable above ground with flexible-hanger provision for normal expansions and contractions.

IMPEDANCES

As a form of conductor that supposedly passes current freely, it would seem that the transmission line would not have an impedance. But at the carrier frequencies the various capacitances between one conductor and the other conductor and between the conductors and ground, as well as the inductive effect of the rapidly alternating current, develop a measurable impedance—the characteristic impedance, Z_o. Another quantity, the *line impedance*, has the same symbol (Z_o) and can be taken as being the ratio of the voltage wave to the current wave traveling along the line. The characteristic impedance is a mutual impedance relating that impedance of the sending or generating end with the receiving-end impedance. Thus, the transmission line and its characteristic impedance become an important part of matching impedances.

Equations to approximate the characteristic impedance for the two-wire line and for the coaxial cable are:

Two-wire line:

$$Z_o = 276 \log_{10} \left(\frac{b}{a} \right) \text{ ohms}$$

Coaxial cable:

$$Z_o = 138 \log_{10} \left(\frac{c}{d} \right) \text{ ohms}$$

where,
a is the conductor radius,
b is the spacing between conductors,
c is the inside radius of the outer conductor,
d is the radius of the inner conductor.

IMPEDANCE MATCHING

A basic rule of electronics states that maximum energy transfer occurs when the load impedance equals the impedance

91

of the generator. In broadcast transmitters, the generator is the carrier power amplifier, while its load is the transmission line and antenna system. Fig. 9-3 shows that the complete system consists of four sections—the carrier amplifier output, the transmission line, and impedance-matching section or net-' work, and the antenna. The junctions between these sections (AA', BB', and CC' of Fig. 9-3) act as two-way mirrors. That is, looking across AA' toward the transmission line, the carrier-amplifier output must "see" a reflection of its own impedance, but the transmission line must "see" through the junction to "see" the same carrier power-amplifier output impedance.

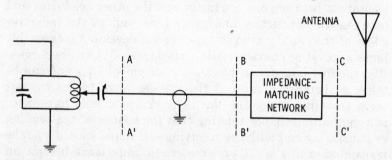

Fig. 9-3. Complete transmitter-to-antenna coupling system.

Characteristic impedance Z_o of the transmission line is the *mutual impedance* between the carrier power amplifier and the impedance-matching network. In turn, the impedance-matching network with a characteristic impedance of Z_o' is the mutual impedance between the antenna and the transmission line. To effect a match, the square of the mutual impedance, Z_m, must equal the product of the impedance on either end of the mutual impedance:

$$Z_m{}^2 = Z'Z''$$

where,
  Z' is the impedance at one end of the mutual impedance,
  Z'' is the impedance at the opposite end of the mutual impedance.

In Fig. 9-3, the transmission-line impedance, Z_o, replaces Z_m of the equation, while Z_p, the carrier power-amplifier output impedance, replaces Z'. Then Z'', the impedance the matching network "sees" looking back into the transmission line, equals

Z_o^2/Z_p. And the matching network must have a characteristic impedance Z_o' that will match Z'', or Z_o^2/Z_p, with the impedance of the antenna, Z_a.

$$Z_o'^2 = Z''Z_a$$
$$= (Z_o^2/Z_p)Z_a$$

If Z_p, the carrier power-amplifier impedance, is 100 ohms, Z_a, the antenna impedance, is 250 ohms, and Z_o, the transmission-line characteristic impedance, is 50 ohms; the required Z_o' of the matching network will be about 80 ohms.

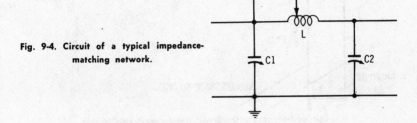

Fig. 9-4. Circuit of a typical impedance-matching network.

IMPEDANCE-MATCHING NETWORK

Fig. 9-4 shows the circuit of a typical impedance-matching network used to match the transmission line to the antenna of a standard broadcast station. As a rule of thumb, the three reactances are each made equal to the desired mutual or characteristic impedance Z_o'; that is, for Z_o' to equal 80 ohms, reactances X_L, X_{C1}, and X_{C2} are made to equal 80 ohms. Then:

$$L = \frac{X_L}{6.28f}$$

$$C1 \text{ and } C2 = \frac{1}{6.28fX_C}$$

and if the frequency, f, is 1000 kHz, inductance L is 12.7 μh, while capacitors C1 and C2 have values of 2000 pf each. Inductance L should be 25 percent larger than this calculated value and then be adjusted by means of a movable shorting tap—its construction is of self-supporting wire or copper tubing. C1 and C2 will also be variable, with maximum values greater than those calculated. Such impedance-matching networks are commonly housed in weathertight cabinets at the base of the antenna tower. In this location the impedance-matching network or a variation of that shown by Fig. 9-4 also eliminates many of the undesirable carrier harmonics.

LINE-MATCHING SECTIONS

At the higher frequencies of the frequency-modulation and television stations, the inductance and capacitance components

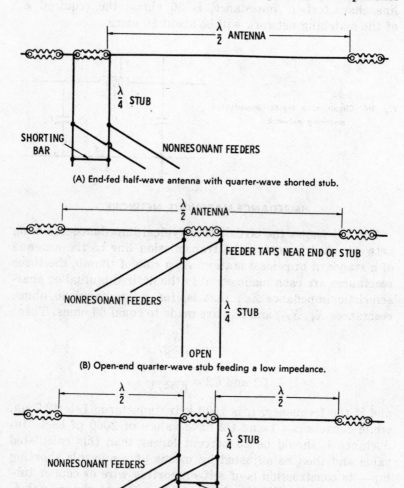

(A) End-fed half-wave antenna with quarter-wave shorted stub.

(B) Open-end quarter-wave stub feeding a low impedance.

(C) Shorted quarter-wave stub feeding voltage to two half-wave antennas.

Fig. 9-5. Methods of using quarter-wavelength sections.

of the impedance-matching network become impractically small. The wavelength has, at these higher frequencies, become short enough that quarter-wavelength sections can be used as matching sections or components of matching sections. A quarter-wavelength section measures 250 feet at 1000 kHz—the standard broadcast range—but 2½ feet is equal to a quarter wavelength at the frequency-modulation frequency of 100 MHz. The theory of the quarter-wavelength section and its usage is rather extensive and will not be given here. However, Fig. 9-5 shows three methods. using quarter-wavelength sections. Since the actual radiating elements of these higher-frequency antennas are located at the top of the tower, the junction between the transmission line and the radiating elements is inaccessible; the impedance-matching section is likely to be located between the carrier power amplifier and the transmission line.

REVIEW QUESTIONS

1. What types of conductors are used to couple the power from the transmitter to the antenna?
2. Name three basic types of transmission lines.
3. What range of characteristic impedances is possible with the two-wire line?
4. Describe the flexible coaxial cable.
5. Why are rigid coaxial cables filled with compressed dry air?
6. Give the equation for the approximate characteristic impedance of a coaxial cable.
7. When does maximum transfer of energy occur?
8. What is the mutual impedance, Z_m, that will match a 50-ohm impedance and a 100-ohm impedance?
9. Determine the values for the inductance and the capacitances of an impedance-matching network having a characteristic impedance of 80 ohms at 1500 kHz.

10

Standard Broadcasting Antennas

Anything that is extremely obvious is often said to "stick out like a sore thumb." Most of the other equipment and facilities of the broadcast station attract very little attention, but the antenna towers are so obvious that they "stick out like a sore thumb." Not so obvious is the relation of these towers with the studios located several miles away in the downtown area. It is not too difficult to understand that the construction or erection of such towers can be complicated in the congested downtown area, but there are many other factors to be considered.

FUNDAMENTALS

The transmitting antenna is primarily a conductor developing a standing wave and radiating both electric-field and magnetic-field waves. A standing wave is produced as the initial wave comes to the end of the conductor and, not being absorbed, is reflected toward the point of origin (see Fig. 1-4). It is this standing wave of current that develops the radiating magnetic waves; the radiating electric-field waves developed by the standing voltage wave are considered to be insignificant. The distribution of this standing current wave depends on the conductor's length in relation to the wavelength, or frequency, of the initial wave. Fig. 10-1 shows the standing-wave distribution for a half-wavelength and a quarter-wavelength conductor.

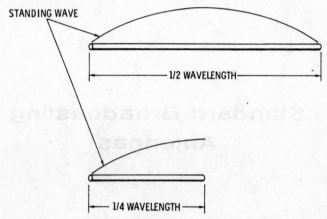

STANDING WAVE

1/2 WAVELENGTH

1/4 WAVELENGTH

Fig. 10-1. Standing-wave distribution for half-wavelength and quarter-wavelength conductors.

Electromagnetic waves radiate perpendicularly to the axis of the conductor. Therefore, there will be little or no radiation from the ends of a conductor. And if the conductor is horizontal —parallel to the earth's surface—the radiation will be bidirectional, as shown by Fig. 10-2A. Fig. 10-2B shows that the radiations from a vertically mounted conductor (perpendicular to the earth's surface) are nondirectional. Thus, a vertical steel tower can readily serve as the radiating conductor. However, the conductor length, expressed in terms of wavelength, affects the amount of radiated wave sent skyward (the sky wave). Although this sky wave may be refracted to earth, the point at which this return to earth occurs will likely be far beyond the primary service area. Accordingly, the sky wave is to be considered as lost radiation and should be kept to a minimum.

Minimum sky wave occurs with a vertical radiator having a height equal to one-half wavelength, but the sky wave is within acceptable limits for tower heights ranging from 0.25 to 0.56 wavelength. At the standard broadcast frequencies, the quarter wavelength (0.25) ranges from 155 to 450 feet, while the half wavelengths (0.5) are 310 to 900 feet. Naturally the taller towers are more costly, and many of the smaller stations use a standard-sized tower—175, 200, 225, 250, etc.—as near the quarter wavelength as possible. Larger and higher-powered stations find it advantageous to use custom-built towers having heights of exactly a half wavelength. For example, clear-channel station WLW in Cincinnati, which has an output power of 50,000 watts, uses a 708-foot tower.

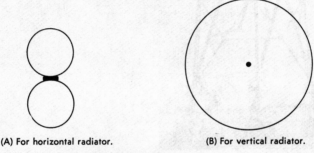

(A) For horizontal radiator.   (B) For vertical radiator.

Fig. 10-2. Radiation patterns.

TOWER CONSTRUCTION

There are two basic types of towers used as radiators or antennas for standard broadcast transmitters—self-supporting and guyed. Self-supporting towers rest upon three or four concrete bases (Fig. 10-3) and are tapered from at least a 10-foot base width to a pointed top. Stranded steel cables provide support for guyed towers resting upon a single base. While it is possible to use a grounded—electrically connected to the earth—antenna tower, most towers are insulated from the earth by a large porcelain insulator. Insulated from the earth, the tall steel tower tends to acquire electrostatic charges, especially during a thunderstorm. A spark gap, not shown distinctly in Fig. 10-3, permits these electrostatic charges to bypass the insulator to ground. The resulting spark also provides a direct path, or "short," to the carrier-signal current and, in turn,

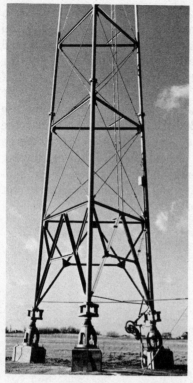

Fig. 10-3. Base of self-supporting tower.

Courtesy WGN, Roselle, Illinois.

allows the power-amplifier anode current to rise to an excessive value that opens the overload relay.

Related to the tower antenna is its associated grounding system. Since the ground, or earth, is in effect the return path of the radiating system, its efficiency depends on the losses produced by the electrical currents in the earth close to the antenna. That is, if the earth near the antenna is highly resistive, a substantial amount of the radiated power will be absorbed, or lost, into the earth. Wires buried in the earth and radiating out from the tower base provide lower-resistance paths for these ground currents. By using 120 such buried wires or radials having lengths equal to 0.5 wavelength, the maximum length of the ground-current path is reduced to less than 0.014 wavelength, a negligible length. Wherever possible this grounding system is also connected to any water source or channel—city water lines, driven wells, tiled or open drainage, creeks, lakes, etc. Actually it is wise to seek out a swampy location for the tower, or even to set the tower into the water of a lake or ocean.

RADIATION PATTERNS

The radiation pattern is the trace, or line, of points receiving equal field intensities. That is, points A, B, and C and all other points on the inner circular pattern of Fig. 10-4 receive a field intensity of 50 millivolts from tower T. Field intensities of 1.0 millivolt are received at points D, E, and F, and all other points on that outer circular pattern. As the radiation patterns of Fig. 10-4 indicate, the radiations of a vertical antenna are nondirectional—meaning that the radiation travels away from the antenna equally in all directions.

However, it is not always practical to radiate the transmitter power equally in all directions. It may be that most of the population to be served is concentrated within an area to one side of the transmitter site. Or it may be that the radiations of two or more stations using the same frequency channels

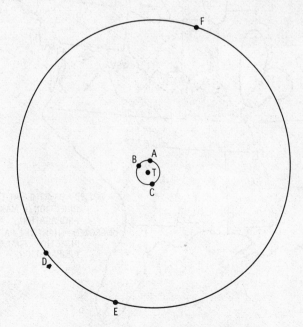

Fig. 10-4. Nondirectional radiation patterns.

will badly interfere if nondirectional antennas are used. As an example, station KSD in St. Louis and station KFRM in Salina, Kansas, each radiate 5000 watts at 550 kilohertz. If both of these stations, about 400 miles apart, had nondirectional antennas, there would likely be considerable interference over much of the area. And while much of this interference area would probably not be commercially important to either KSD or KFRM, it would mean a loss of power to each. Therefore, KFRM uses an array of three towers to throw its radiation to the southwest in the daytime while KSD uses a nondirectional antenna (Fig. 10-5). KFRM does not operate at night,

DOTTED = DAYTIME PATTERN OR
DIRECTION OF MAXIMUM
PROPAGATION.
UNBROKEN = NIGHTTIME PATTERN OR
DIRECTION OF MAXIMUM
PROPAGATION.

Fig. 10-5. Radiation patterns of stations operating at 550 kHz.

but KSD is also concerned with the interference of WKRC at Cincinnati. So at night, KSD limits its radiation to the north and west. At the same time, WKRC is involved with radiations from WSVA, at Harrisonburg, Virginia, also operating on the 550-kHz channel. And so it goes across the nation as over 1000 standard broadcast stations use the 105 channels between 550 and 1600 kHz.

TOWER ARRAYS

To direct the radiations toward a particular area or direction, more than one antenna tower is used. With these towers spaced at specified distances and fed with carrier voltages that are out of phase, the radiation pattern is shaped to the desired form. Fig. 10-6 illustrates a simple two-tower array. Tower T1 is a quarter wavelength from tower T2 and is fed by a carrier current that lags the carrier current fed to tower T2 by a quar-

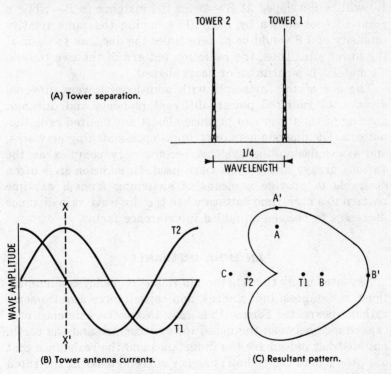

(A) Tower separation.

(B) Tower antenna currents.

(C) Resultant pattern.

Fig. 10-6. Two-tower arrangement.

ter cycle. That is, when the radiations leaving tower T1 are at a positive maximum, those of tower T2 will be zero, going negative (time XX' of Fig. 10-6B). Reception point A is about equidistant from T1 and T2 (Fig. 10-6C). The two radiations arrive at A one quarter of a wavelength out of phase, adding to achieve a field intensity of 1.414 times that produced by radiations from a single tower. In the next situation, the radiations from tower T2 travel a quarter wavelength farther than those from tower T1, and the radiations are in phase as they arrive at point B, adding to achieve twice the field intensity from a single tower. At point C, the two signals arrive 180 degrees out of phase, and the resultant is a field intensity of zero.

Since the field intensity is inversely proportional to distance, if the distance to A' is 1.414 times the distance to A, the field intensity at A' will be 1.0 times that produced by radiations from a single tower. In the same way, a relative intensity of 1.0 will be developed at B'—twice the distance to B—while a point C' (not shown by Fig. 10-6) having the same relative intensity of 1.0 would be at zero times the distance to C, or at the tower site. Thus, the radiation pattern of the two towers, T1 and T2, is a cardioid, or heart shaped.

The use of this principle with additional towers, unequal division of radiated power, different phasing, and different spacing of the tower can produce almost any desired radiation pattern. The phasing networks, impedance-matching networks, and transmission-line systems become very complex as the various arrays and patterns are used. In addition it is often desirable to provide a means of switching from a daytime pattern to a nighttime pattern when the sky-wave skip distance decreases to become an added interference factor.

ANTENNA IMPEDANCE

As stated many times before, in radio-frequency communications, resistances, inductances, and capacitances acquire some rather unexpected forms. It is easy to see the existence of a capacitance between the metal tower structure and the earth, but abstract indeed are the inductance and the resistance that are products of the radio-frequency current. That is, the rapid alternations of the radio-frequency currents cause reactions to be developed. The net effect of the physical impedances and the abstract reactions is an impedance having both a resistance component and a reactance component—either an inductive reactance or a capacitive reactance.

Since the ground, earth, is a portion of the antenna system and its impedance, that impedance must be determined by actual measurement at the tower site. A signal generator— small transmitter—is coupled to the antenna to give a convenient current meter (M) reading (see Fig. 10-7) with switch S closed. Then, with switch S open, the standard or calibrated impedance Z_s is adjusted until meter M reads half its initial value. Reduction of the current read by meter M to half value indicates that the impedance has been doubled and that the calibrated impedance, Z_s, equals that of the antenna. With tower arrays, a measurement is necessary for each tower.

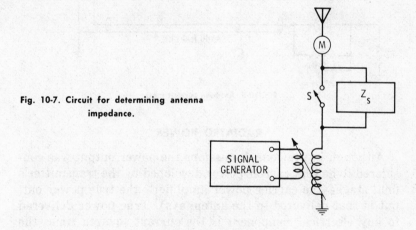

Fig. 10-7. Circuit for determining antenna impedance.

ANTENNA CURRENT

At the base of the antenna, usually in the same cabinet or housing as the impedance-matching network, a thermocouple-type ammeter indicates the true effective value of r-f current being fed into that antenna (Fig. 10-8). A switch (not shown) removes the meter from the circuit when not being read. If the antenna tower is close to the transmitter building, the transmission line will be short and the line current nearly the same as the antenna current. However, the building is seldom built that close to an antenna, so a remote antenna current meter is necessary. Inductance L in Fig. 10-8 has a sampling voltage induced in it by the antenna current; the induced voltage in turn develops a current carried by the sampling line to meter M2 within the transmitter building. R1, the adjustable shunt resistance across meter M2, serves to adjust the reading of M2 to agree with antenna current meter M1. Resistance R2 acts as a load matching the sampling line and circuit. The voltage developed across R2 will also serve as a sampling for phase monitoring where a tower array is used. A separate antenna current meter and remote antenna current meter are necessary for each tower.

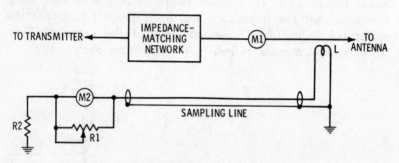

Fig. 10-8. Antenna current meter.

RADIATED POWER

Although in previous discussions the power output was considered to be that carrier power developed by the transmitter's final stage—the carrier power amplifier—the true power output is that delivered to the antenna(s). True power delivered to any electrical component is the current squared times the resistance. This resistance is that resistive component of the antenna impedance, Z_a, where

$$Z_a{}^2 = R_a{}^2 + X_a{}^2$$

The power output, P_o, is

$$P_o = I_a{}^2 R_a$$

With tower arrays, the total power output is the sum of the powers radiated by each tower:

$$P_o = P_1 + P_2 + P_3 + \ldots$$

And since FCC regulations state that the radiated power shall not be over 5 percent above the assigned value and not more than 10 percent below that assigned value, the antenna current must be maintained between 0.95 and 1.023 of that value producing the assigned power value. Using the equation

$$I_a = \sqrt{\frac{R_a}{P_o}}$$

if P_o is to be 1000 watts and the antenna resistance is 216 ohms, the normal antenna current should be 2.15 amperes, but can vary between 2.04 and 2.20 amperes.

REVIEW QUESTIONS

1. Does an antenna develop a standing wave?
2. Is the distribution of the standing wave dependent on the length in relation to the frequency?
3. Are the radiations from a horizontally mounted antenna bidirectional or nondirectional?
4. Is the sky wave economically important to the standard broadcast station?
5. Name the two types of antenna towers. Are these towers usually grounded?
6. Why is a spark gap built onto an antenna tower?
7. Why are wires buried in the ground surrounding an antenna tower? Are towers ever located out in the water of a lake?
8. Define the radiation pattern.
9. Give two reasons why nondirectional radiation may not be practical.
10. Why are tower arrays used?
11. Does the antenna impedance include a reactance?
12. Why is a remote antenna current meter necessary?
13. What variation is permitted in the radiated power? In the antenna current?

11

F-M and Television Antennas

We are often reminded of the great advancements made in our methods of transportation. But with the changes in vehicles, the highways have also been improved. The fact is that our modern automobiles would find it almost impossible to maneuver on the roads of yesteryear. The antique-auto hobbyist often must make minor alterations to adjust his horseless carriage to the modern highway. In a like manner, the carrier frequencies for frequency modulation and television broadcasting require conductors and antennas differing from the tower radiators of standard broadcast stations.

FUNDAMENTALS

Unlike the waves of the lower standard broadcast frequencies, those of frequency modulation and television broadcasts remain oriented to their original plane and do not bend. That is, a high-frequency wave radiated from a vertical antenna (vertically polarized) must be received from a vertical

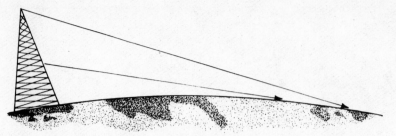

Fig. 11-1. Effect of height on line-of-sight transmission.

antenna, and those waves travel in straight lines rather than bending around buildings, mountains, or the curvature of the earth. Known as line-of-sight transmission, the limit of reception of the waves is the horizon. But by adding height the horizon—line of sight—is pushed farther away (see Fig. 11-1). Fortunately, with these higher-frequency waves the dimensions af a half-wave or quarter-wave radiating element are small enough to permit placement high atop a building or tower.

BASIC ANTENNA TYPE

The basic radiating element used for f-m and television broadcasting is the half-wave dipole—two wires or rods separated and fed at the center (Fig. 11-12). Another form of half-wave antenna is a single rod fed from each end (Fig. 11-3). When the half-wave dipole is mounted vertically, so that as we look down on it as we see only the rod end, its radiation is non-directional (Fig. 10-2B). But with horizontal mounting (Fig. 10-2A) the radiation is bidirectional. A three-dimensional form of these combined radiation patterns looks much like a dough-nut. Nondirectional patterns are achieved by crossing two hori-

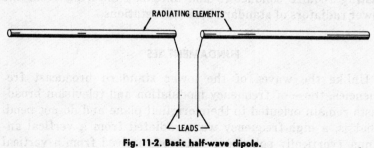

RADIATING ELEMENTS

LEADS

Fig. 11-2. Basic half-wave dipole.

Fig. 11-3. Half-wave antenna fed from
each end.

zontally mounted half-wave elements (Fig. 11-4A) or by bending a single half-wave element into a circle (Fig. 11-4B). The actual mechanical form of the half-wave elements varies considerably.

For the uhf television channels, 14 to 83 (470 to 890 MHz), the radiating antenna takes on the appearance of a tube having a number of slots cut into its surface (Fig. 11-5). The modulated carrier waves are brought up through the tube by a transmission line (or wave guide) and coupled to that tube at the various slot levels. However, the high r-f resistance and impedance of this solid steel tube will concentrate the currents at the slot edges. Standing waves and radiations are then developed along the edges of each slot.

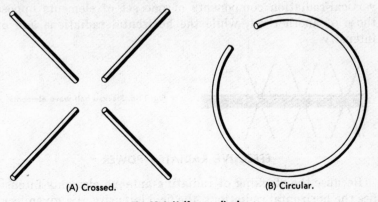

(A) Crossed.   (B) Circular.

Fig. 11-4. Half-wave dipoles.

SLOTS

Fig. 11-5. Slotted antenna for uhf broadcasting.

ELEMENT STACKING

Radiations in the vertical plane are nondirectional for a horizontally mounted antenna element, meaning that a considerable portion of the radiation is sent skyward. Such very high- or ultrahigh-frequency sky waves are lost and serve no purpose because they are not bent, or refracted, back to earth as lower-frequency waves are sometimes. Reduction of these sky waves and intensification of the ground wave are accomplished by stacking two or more of these radiating elements above each other. Fig. 11-6 shows three crossed half-wave elements stacked on a center support with a spacing, commonly one wavelength, between each set of elements. In this manner, vertical-radiation components of one set of elements oppose those of another set, while the horizontal radiations add or intensify.

Fig. 11-6. Stacked half-wave elements.

EFFECTIVE RADIATED POWER

Because the stacking of radiating-antenna elements intensifies the horizontal radiations, the field intensity at a given location is increased. If the relative field intensity, E, follows the equation

$$E = \frac{186.4\sqrt{P}}{d}$$

it is as though the power, P (transmitter power), has been increased to an effective radiated power P'. This effective radiated power P' develops the increased field intensity at the given distance, d:

$$P' = \frac{(E'd)^2}{186.4}$$

Effective radiated power P' is actually dependent on the number of radiating elements in the stacked system. For example, suppose that a stacked system of three elements has a power gain, G, of 3.1. Then, if the transmitter is developing a power P of 10,000 watts, the effective radiated power P' is 31,000 watts ($3.1 \times 10,000$). With a stack of 12 elements, a power gain of about 11.0 will increase a transmitter power P of 10,000 watts to an effective radiated power P' of 110,000 watts. Thus the new effective radiated power is $P' = GP$.

POWER DETERMINATION

F-m and television transmitting antenna systems do have an impedance and a resistance component. However, at the top of a tower, measurement of that antenna resistance or the antenna current is impractical. In fact, it is almost impossible to obtain a true measurement of current at these frequencies. A common method of measuring vhf and uhf power uses the comparison of heat or light produced by the unknown power with that produced by a known quantity of power.

Fig. 11-7 shows the output of a transmitter coupled to a group of light bulbs. A light meter like that used in photograpy is placed close enough to one of the light bulbs to obtain a convenient reading. Then switch S is reversed so that the bulbs are fed from the 60-hertz power source or from a direct-current source. Resistance R is adjusted until the light meter, in the same location as before, is again reading the same as with the transmitter power. Of course, switch S should be reversed several times to make certain the light meter does

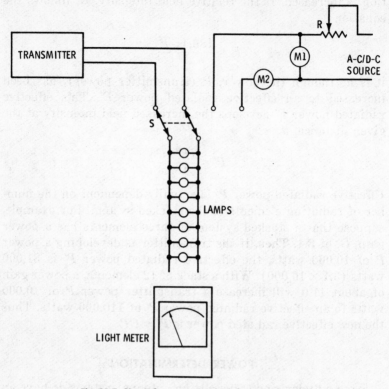

Fig. 11-7. Circuit for measuring high-frequency power.

have the same reading in either position. P, the transmitter power, is then taken to be equal to the product of the voltage, V, and the current, I, indicated by meters M1 and M2. This method is limited in the amount of power that can be measured and by the inaccuracy introduced through impedance mismatching. However, a transmission-line section can be utilized as an impedance-matching device, while some heat absorption and measuring methods can extend the range of measured power. There are commercially built "dummy" loads having the same 50-ohm impedance as the transmission lines and antenna, plus a calibrated watt-meter. Such "dummy" loads have resistance units immersed in a liquid coolant that is in turn cooled by moving water.

None of the above methods of determining power output can be used during actual program broadcasting, but they do provide a means of calibrating the transmitter output meter. When the "dummy" load and meters indicate that the output power is at the desired level, the transmitter output meter—inductively coupled to the transmission line—is adjusted to read 100 percent. With the two transmitters (video and audio) of the television station, it is necessary to determine the power output and to calibrate the output meter of each.

DIPLEXERS

The television station radiates two carrier signals, one for the video modulating signal and a second to carry the sound, or audio, modulating signal. To couple the two carrier signals

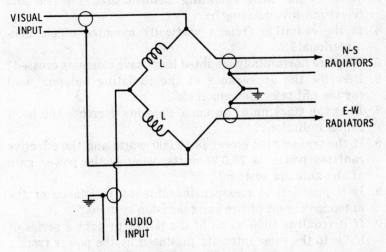

Fig. 11-8. Bridge-circuit equivalent of diplexer.

to one antenna system, some form of mixer is needed. One basic form of mixer is the bridge (Fig. 11-8), a form of the Wheatstone bridge. However, in this case the bridge mixer—the *diplexer*—is a combination of transmission-line segments. The output arms of the bridge, or diplexer, represents the crossed half-wave dipoles being fed by currents that are 90 degrees out of phase. That is, dipoles set in the north-south direction are fed by a current which is 90 degrees out of phase with that fed to those dipoles having an east-west position. While the crossed dipoles are commonly fed in this manner—

115

out of phase—there may be situations where this would not be true and the diplexer would be arranged for a single output.

Dimensions of the diplexer depend on the channel and frequency, but the overall length of a commercially built type is less than 10 feet, and it can be located at any position between the transmitter and the antenna tower.

REVIEW QUESTIONS

1. Do the waves radiated by f-m and television stations bend around the curvature of the earth?
2. What is the limit of reception for television signals? Why are the radiating elements placed on high towers?
3. What is the basic radiating element used for f-m and television broadcasting?
4. Is the radiation from a vertically mounted dipole non-directional?
5. Why are horizontally mounted half-wave elements crossed?
6. Describe the appearance of the radiating antenna used for the uhf television channels.
7. Does the stacking of antenna elements decrease the horizontal radiations?
8. If the transmitter power is 10,000 watts and the effective radiated power is 76,000 watts, what is the power gain of the antenna system?
9. Is it practical to measure the antenna resistance or the antenna current of f-m and television systems?
10. If it requires 1000 watts of d-c power to light a series of bulbs to the same intensity produced by the power from a transmitter, what is the transmitter output power?

12

Remote Transmitter Operating

While we continue to be amazed by the clockwork precision of nature, man can also be proud of the accuracy he has built into many of his machines. One of the most outstanding examples is the electronic computer—its accuracy often being far beyond that of which man himself is capable. In broadcasting, the factor of accuracy is replaced by reliability and stability. Fortunately, the reliability and stability of most broadcast equipment are very good. With a regular schedule—usually weekly—of preventive maintenance, the standard-broadcast or frequency-modulation transmitter will require little or no adjustment. This means that the transmitter operator is occupied mostly with reading the meters and keeping a record, the log. But if these meter readings can be made from the studio control room, the studio engineer can also act as transmitter engineer.

REQUIRED READINGS

Federal Communication Commission regulations state that within every half-hour during the broadcasting time, readings must be taken and received for the carrier power amplifier's anode voltage and anode current, antenna current or power output level, and the frequency or frequency deviation. In addition, the individual station engineer may want a record of other factors—filament voltages, grid and anode currents of stages preceding the carrier power amplifier, transmission-line current, and crystal and other various temperatures. While the FCC does not require the recording of these other factors, they can often provide an indication of expected trouble.

BASIC REMOTE-TRANSMITTER OPERATING SYSTEM

An initial requirement of a remote-transmitter system is a means of switching the filament power and the anode power on and off. Use of a telephone line provides the connecting link between the transmitter and its remote operating panel. While circuits may differ greatly, that of Fig. 12-1 will serve to start and to stop the filament power and the anode power.

Resistors R1, R2, R3, R4, and R5 serve as a voltage-dividing network, dividing the voltage of battery B1 and setting the normal voltage between point A and the ground at point C or C′ just slightly more than half the voltage of B1. This normal voltage, between A and C′, produces a current through relays K1 and K2 that will not pull down their armatures, but that will hold these armatures down after they have been pulled down. When pushbutton S4 is pressed, the current is increased to pull down the armature of K1, but not K2, to feed the 110-volt alternating current into the primaries of the filament transformers and, via diode D1, pulses of half-wave rectified alternating current into transformer T2 and thus to transformer T1. Diode D2 passes these pulses of rectified alternating current to activate relay K3 and light the associated (green) indicator lamp.

Operation of switch S3 provides still greater direct current to close the contacts of relay K2, feeding 110 volts alternating current, or three-phase 220-volt voltages, to the high-voltage transformer(s), starting the anode power. The closing of the

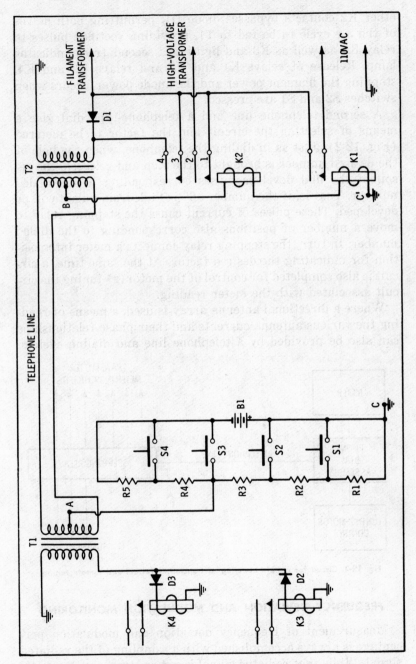

Fig. 12-1. Remote system for starting and stopping filament power and anode power.

other K2 contacts bypasses diode D1, permitting both halves of the a-c cycle to be fed to T1, providing rectified pulses to relay K4 as well as K3 and lighting a second (red) indicator lamp. Release of relays K1 and K3 and relays K2 and K4, stopping the filament power and the anode power, occurs when switches S2 and S1 are pressed.

A second telephone line and a telephone-type dial give a means of selecting the circuit and the factor to be metered (Fig. 12-2). Just as in dialing the telephone, when the hole of the desired number is brought to the stop and released, the re-coil of the dial develops pulses corresponding to the dialed number. That is, if the number "6" is dialed, six pulses will be developed. These pulses of current cause the stepping relay to move a number of positions also corresponding to the dialed number. In turn, the stepping relay connects a meter into position for indicating the desired factor. At the same time, a cir-cuit is also completed for control of the motor(s) tuning the cir-cuit associated with the meter reading.

Where a directional antenna array is used, a means of read-ing the various antenna currents and their phase relationships can also be provided by a telephone line and dialing system.

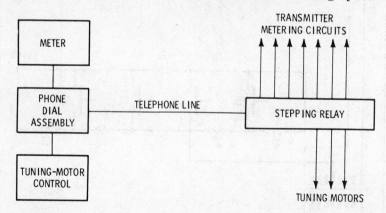

Fig. 12-2. Circuit for remote metering of transmitter factors and remote tuning.

FREQUENCY DEVIATION AND MODULATION MONITORING

Measurement of frequency deviation and modulation per-centage is always accomplished with a sampling of the radiated signal. While that radiated signal is not as strong at the studio control room as at the transmitter site, it *is* present at the studio and can be monitored. Amplification of the modulated carrier wave received at the studio central room may be necessary before the usual monitor will function.

REVIEW QUESTIONS

1. According to FCC regulations what readings must be taken from the broadcasting transmitter within every half-hour of broadcasting time?
2. What readings, in addition to the FCC-required ones, might a broadcasting station engineer also want?
3. Is preventive maintenance at the broadcast station usually daily, weekly, or monthly?
4. What connects the transmitter with its remote operating panel?
5. Can the radiated signal be practically monitored at the studio?

Answers to
Review Questions

CHAPTER 1

1. When a conductor moves through a magnetic field, or a magnetic field varies about a conductor, an electric current is induced into the conductor. No, a direct current will not develop the necessary varying magnetic field.

2. Wavelength is the measure of the distance traveled by a wave during the time of one cycle. 300 meters.

3. A standing wave is the result of an initial wave and a reflected wave along a transmission line or other conductor.

4. Electromagnetic and electrostatic.

5. About 30 miles. Less than 50 miles.

6. The modulating signal is the intelligence, or load, placed on a radio-frequency wave. The modulated wave is the radio-frequency wave with the modulating signal.

7. No.

CHAPTER 2

1. Audio or sound waves are the result of vibrations producing waves of air that give the sensation of sound.

2. A device to change audio waves into electrical waves or electrical waves into audio waves. Microphones, phonograph pickups, and tape-recording devices.

3. No.

4. Transcription recordings are disc recordings with a 16-inch diameter, four to six musical numbers on each side, and cut from the center out at 33⅓ rpm.

5. 7½ inches per second.
6. For the playing of short announcements, commercials, etc.
7. For remote and network programming as well as connecting the audio studio with the transmitter.
8. Preamplifiers, program amplifier, monitor amplifier.
9. The control console consists of a sloping front panel having the switches, attenuators, and meters needed for proper control of the audio system.
10. Balanced.
11. The vu meter is a rectifier-type voltmeter used to indicate the volume or amplitude level of the audio signal. 0.001 watt across 600 ohms or 1 volume unit.
12. A patch panel is a series of jacks prearranged for temporary repair or alterations of audio equipment.

CHAPTER 3

1. None. No.
2. Silver salts turn black in the presence of white light.
3. The electronic retina has a surface of minute photosensitive globules insulated from a metal backplate. Very positive.
4. Scanning is the movement, horizontally and vertically, of the eyes or the electron beam over an image. The purpose of the horizontal pulses is to move the electron beam from side to side. Vertical pulses move the beam up and down.
5. 30. 525.
6. 4.5 MHz.
7. Locating and focusing of the image on the electronic retina.
8. Adjust the sharpness of the electron beam.

9. 10 inches per second.
10. The projectors are arranged with mirrors or prisms to project directly into the lens of a camera.
11. A telephone line will not carry the 4.5-MHz frequency range of the video modulating signal.
12. American Telephone and Telegraph and the local phone companies.
13. Direct coupling.
14. To provide a visual check of the scanning pulses.
15. So that both the transmitting and the receiving processes will be stable.
16. No, the pulses developed by the synchronization signal generator have a rounded or sawtooth form.

CHAPTER 4

1. The carrier wave of r-f wave has a frequency that develops sufficient standing wave and radiation, and little or no frequency range.
2. 88 to 108 MHz.
3. 10,000 Hz. 200 kHz. 6 MHz.
4. An oscillator.
5. The capacitance between the grid and the anode of the oscillator tube. Its dimensions.
6. To maintain its dimensions and the frequency. 75°C.
7. The buffer stage. The buffer is a tuned r-f amplifier having a very low amplification, lessening the effect of a load upon the oscillator.
8. Tuned r-f amplifier having the anode circuit tuned to a multiple of the grid frequency. 98.1 MHz.
9. To provide a continuous means of measuring carrier-frequency deviations. Sampling loop, r-f

amplifier, crystal oscillator, discriminator. Yes. At the center.

CHAPTER 5

1. That area being adequately served by a broadcast station. 8 to 1.
2. Doubled.
3. Class C.
4. To lessen the possibility of undesired oscillations.
5. The carrier power amplifier must be linear to follow the variations induced by modulation.
6. Prevention of oscillations.
7. Oscillator, modulator, buffer, multipliers.
8. No, most resonant circuits are tuned by electric motors.
9. Anode voltage, anode current, and the output or the antenna current.
10. Heat. Fins are added to radiate the heat away from the tube.

CHAPTER 6

1. Audio power amplifier. Within the anode circuit.
2. When the audio or video signal has a peak value equal to the anode power supply.
3. The ratio of half the difference between the maximum and minimum amplitudes to the amplitude of the unmodulated carrier. The modulation percentage is given by

$$M = \frac{(H - K) \times 100}{2C}$$

where,
   M is the modulation percenttage,
   H is the maximum amplitude of the modulated wave,
   K is the minimum amplitude of the modulated wave,
   C is the amplitude of the unmodulated wave.

4. Overmodulation results when the negative half-cycle of the audio or video signal swings beyond the anode-current cutoff limit.
5. The modulated current is 1.23 times the unmodulated value. Modulated power is 1.5 times the unmodulated power.
6. 2500 watts.
7. Yes. The carrier amplitude. 0 to 133 percent.
8. No.
9. No.

CHAPTER 7

1. Frequency modulation is the change of frequency according to the amplitude of the audio signal.
2. No.
3. The capacitor microphone is made a part of the oscillator resonant tuned circuit so that sound waves alter the capacitance and frequency.
4. The reactance tube adds inductive or capacitive reactance.
5. Phase modulation alters the time relationships of the carrier wave. Yes.
6. Phasitron. No. By means of an external winding or magnetic coil.
7. Direct crystal control of center frequency, modulation independent of frequency control, low distortion, low noise level, simplicity of circuit and circuit alignment (*any three*).
8. 88 percent.
9. To compensate for the inadequacies of many f-m receivers.

CHAPTER 8

1. The electric utility. The three-phase system consists of three

alternating voltage (currents) spaced or timed ⅓ cycle apart.
2. 165 kilowatts.
3. Rectifiers are devices which pass current readily in one direction while opposing current passage in the opposite direction. 120 hertz.
4. 180 Hz. 360 Hz.
5. No.
6. The secondary winding of a variable transformer is constructed about a semicircular iron core moving in and out of the stationary primary winding.
7. To eliminate the possibility of excessive currents.
8. To avoid the possibility of electrical shock.

CHAPTER 9

1. Transmission lines.
2. Two-wire line, flexible coaxial cable, rigid coaxial cable.
3. 200 to 800 ohms.
4. Flexible coaxial cables have a stranded inner conductor separated from the braided outer conductor by a layer of plastic and an overall vinyl jacket.
5. To keep out moisture.
6. $Z_o = 138 \log_{10}(c/d)$ ohms.
7. When the load impedance equals the impedance of the generator.
8. 70 ohms.
9. L equals 8.47 μh. C1 and C2 equal 1325 pf.

CHAPTER 10

1. Yes.
2. Yes.
3. Bidirectional.
4. No.
5. Self-supporting and guyed. No.
6. To permit electrostatic charges to bypass the insulator to ground.

7. To give lower resistance paths for ground currents. Yes.
8. The trace, or line, of points receiving equal field intensities.
9. Unbalanced concentration of population and undesirable interference from other stations.
10. To direct radiations toward a particular area or direction.
11. Yes.
12. Because the transmitter building is seldom built close to the antenna tower.
13. Not more than 5 percent above and not more than 10 percent below. Between 0.95 and 1.023 of that antenna current producing the assigned power value.

CHAPTER 11

1. No.
2. The horizon. To push the horizon farther away.
3. Half-wave dipole.
4. Yes.
5. To achieve nondirectional patterns.
6. Appears as a tube having slots cut into its surface.
7. No, it decreases the vertical radiations.
8. 7.6.
9. No.
10. 1000 watts.

CHAPTER 12

1. Carrier power amplifier's anode voltage and anode current, antenna current or output power level, and frequency deviation.
2. Filament voltage, grid and anode currents of stages preceding the carrier power amplifier, transmission-line current, crystal and other temperatures.
3. Weekly.
4. A telephone line.
5. Yes.

Index